The Choice Maker

— HAMID RAFIZADEH —

ARCHWAY
PUBLISHING

This book is a work of non-fiction. Unless otherwise noted, the author and the publisher make no explicit guarantees as to the accuracy of the information contained in this book and in some cases, names of people and places have been altered to protect their privacy.

Scripture taken from the King James Version of the Bible.

Archway Publishing books may be ordered through booksellers or by contacting:

Archway Publishing
1663 Liberty Drive
Bloomington, IN 47403
www.archwaypublishing.com
1 (888) 242-5904

Because of the dynamic nature of the Internet, any web addresses or links contained in this book may have changed since publication and may no longer be valid. The views expressed in this work are solely those of the author and do not necessarily reflect the views of the publisher, and the publisher hereby disclaims any responsibility for them.

Any people depicted in stock imagery provided by Getty Images are models, and such images are being used for illustrative purposes only. Certain stock imagery © Getty Images.

ISBN: 978-1-4808-6247-0 (sc)
ISBN: 978-1-4808-6246-3 (e)

Library of Congress Control Number: 2018905044

Print information available on the last page.

Archway Publishing rev. date: 05/21/2018

Contents

I

Quick, Make an Introduction

In the beginning the Sermon on the Mount is not an easy subject because we have never studied it. It is as if I am putting you through grade school again. Do you like that? I doubt it. Neither do I. But as we well know, we must complete it if we are to move toward a good life. My elementary focus in the Sermon on the Mount—the grade school equivalent if you will—is on the beatitudes, primarily the first four verses. Common tradition divides the eight beatitudes into two sets of four. In each set, the end is highlighted by the key word "righteousness."[1] The first set is about daily life while the second moves the daily life in the direction of perfection. Perfection lies in a distant horizon, so in this school the focus remains on the first four beatitudes which are:[2]

> [3] Blessed are the poor in spirit: for theirs is the kingdom of heaven.

 [4] Blessed are they that mourn: for they shall be comforted.

 [5] Blessed are the meek: for they shall inherit the earth.

 [6] Blessed are they which do hunger and thirst after righteousness: for they shall be filled.

The beatitudes set a simple and compact view of life, though in the early stages of grade school learning, one would not have a clear conception of their significance and importance to human life. At first glance, defining, summarizing, and conceptualizing the complete human existence in four seemingly simple statements seems a bit impossible and outrageous. Nonetheless, I start with the common consensus of religious scholars that the first beatitude occupies the core and is basic to understanding the Sermon on the Mount in its entirety. It is noted "this beatitude is not only the first in order, but also the one that in some way generates all others."[3] I have adopted the same perspective.

More on the first beatitude

Despite its centrality and apparent simplicity, the first beatitude has always seemed beyond human understanding. The challenge has existed since its first appearance and lies in the Greek words translated literally as "poor in spirit." What does "poor in spirit" mean? Here is part of the difficulty. This expression is "unique in the entire New Testament and does not appear at all in the early Christian literature or elsewhere in the Greek language."[4] The singular uniqueness could be one reason why the "poor in spirit" has been interpreted in radically different ways. The Greek words can be translated into English in alternative interpretations. For example, we can see it as real economic poverty or lacking—not having "spirit." [5]

Consider the lacking—not having "spirit." What is "spirit"? What is this thing that we lack? The traditional view interprets the key feature of "spirit" as *giver* of gifts of wisdom, knowledge, healing, etc., all attributes of a "knowledge giver."[6] All knowledge giving in human life is built on knowledge seeking and knowledge sharing. If one does not seek knowledge and does not engage in knowledge sharing, one would not be capable of knowledge giving. We can see the combination of knowledge seeking and knowledge sharing as "knowledge processing" or more generally as "knowledge management." This makes the human the "knowledge manager." As knowledge manager the human has to engage in knowledge seeking, knowledge sharing, knowledge processing, and knowledge giving if one is to exist. So the first divine instruction is basically the question, "Can you see you're poor as knowledge giver?" This in turn implies, "Can you see you're poor as knowledge seeker?" and "Can you see you're poor as knowledge sharer?" as well as "Can you see you're poor as knowledge processor?"

From my own life experience, none of this comes as a surprise. I am of the opinion that none of this should come as a surprise to any human. We are poor—really poor—in knowledge giving. Instead we are super in delivering bull and pretending to be know-it-alls in every subject. The divine says we would be "happy"—blessed—if we could see ourselves as being bad in "knowledge giving" because that recognition would direct our attention back to knowledge seeking and knowledge sharing so that we would become better knowledge givers.

Where did the "happy" enter the scene in place of the "blessed"? The Greek word translated as "blessed" can also be translated as "happy."[7] Religion prefers to use the word "blessed" as it places the credit for achievement of happiness on an imaginary "other" that does the blessing. In contrast, the word "happy" makes the human individual the achiever of the happiness through recognizing and addressing the knowledge-giving deficiencies.

In every society on earth, for thousands of years, the starting point of life has always been in "management of brute force" and not in "improving knowledge giving." Anywhere in the world, before any knowledge giving is done, we are keenly interested in setting up the force-based boundaries around us. This is the first significant difference. The divine suggests we start with recognition of poor knowledge giving—poor knowledge seeking and knowledge sharing—and not with brute force and boundary drawing.

Every human capability—in every job, every interaction, and in every situation—originates in one's competence and skill in knowledge giving. Every society is founded and maintained by those that share their capabilities with others and are capable of giving knowledge to others. The human societies exist through "sharing of capabilities," the shared knowledge giving. Every human being should know that fact of life for the simple reason that all goods and services used in daily life are "knowledge-packets," combinations of human knowledge and earth material originating at shared capabilities. The divine being, however, goes one more step to make us aware that we're not good at knowledge giving.

Why do we need a divine reminder? Is it because we never see ourselves as "knowledge deficient?" We need to think about this. If we were good, or at least not bad in seeing where we stand in relation to knowledge seeking and knowledge sharing, the divine would not see a need to remind us. But we are reminded. A divine being sees the need to remind us of knowledge-based ways that improve the human societies' capability sharing. Getting better in capability sharing—getting better in knowledge giving, knowledge seeking, and knowledge sharing—is the only way to advance human well-being and existence.

But none of this sounds familiar or right. Starting with myself, if I am declared a deficient "knowledge giver" I arrive at the inevitable troubling conclusion that I am "knowledge deficient." I don't like that. I don't like being called "knowledge deficient." Why? I don't know. This is no different than someone telling me I am terrible at playing tennis. I know I am awful in tennis, but I don't like being told so. In my experience, no one likes being called "knowledge deficient." We all come with the mindset that what we already know is "a lot" and if we are missing any knowledge it is minor and only at the edges of what we know. Yet being "poor in knowledge giving" can readily imply "being knowledge deficient." We must ask what that means. If humans know they are "knowledge deficient" what will they do? If they listen to the divine, check themselves and recognize they are poor in knowledge giving—if they see the correspondence to knowledge deficiency—how should they address their shortcomings?

If aware of being poor in knowledge-giving, humans would engage in two distinct behaviors. First, each individual would have to become an avid "knowledge seeker." This would increase each individual's knowledge base but such behavior does little to address the overall knowledge deficiency. I am a business professor and I can seek knowledge to become a better business professor, but regardless of how hard I try, I will not have the knowledge to make my own food, my own car, my own computer, my own pharmaceuticals, and many other things I need in life. The only way I can address such deep knowledge deficiency is through "knowledge sharing"—founded on the knowledge giving acts of other humans. Thus, the second thing every human needs to do is to become an avid "knowledge sharer." If every human becomes an avid knowledge seeker and knowledge sharer, the life becomes more *happy*.

The awareness of poor knowledge giving as "knowledge deficiency" results in humans acting as <u>knowledge seeker</u> and <u>knowledge sharer</u> in order to improve the human condition as <u>knowledge giver</u>. Why is this important? The act of sharing sets up the "societal sharing system." It is the societal sharing system that provides everyone with goods and services for their daily needs. The better we share, the more able we are to get what we need in life.

An important aspect of the first beatitude therefore is that knowledge giving—knowledge seeking and knowledge sharing—makes the divine teaching universal, applicable to every human and every aspect of life. Throughout history this type of "universality" has been scary to religion. Being highly selective, no religion can accept the divine teaching that goes beyond the religious boundaries to include everyone in the world. In the Sermon on the Mount, there is no prerequisite before one becomes aware of "knowledge deficiency" in human life, before one engages in knowledge seeking and knowledge sharing in order to address the poor knowledge giving. There is no demand that one should have a certain religious orientation or be a member of certain religious organizations before one can start recognizing one is poor in knowledge giving. It applies to anyone without any preconditions.

Another intriguing feature of the Sermon on the Mount and especially the beatitudes is the "conditionality" of the teaching. There is no statement that everyone *must* do it, nor if anyone does not they are destined for hell. All such threats are built into the boundaries drawn by every religion in order to maintain and protect the religion's believers. Without such boundaries the religion cannot exist. Yet there are no such boundaries in the Sermon on the Mount. There are no musts. There are no threats. There is only the divine being teaching and the human having the choice (the freewill) of using or not using the divine knowledge.

Does this mean the Sermon on the Mount is a destroyer of religions and unifier of humankind? The divine would laugh at that notion and see it as a sign of not understanding the human as "choice maker." The human can choose any religion and to that choice add or not add the Sermon on the Mount. The human can remain Catholic, Baptist, Moslem, Hindu, Buddhist, and any other of thousands of variations and also choose to add or not add the Sermon on the Mount as way of life. The Sermon on the Mount is not a religion. It is only a message from the divine for a way of life that best suits the human in the transition between the earth's two versions.[8] The divine wants to give the human the best chance of survival when facing the transition between the earth's two versions and the best chance to keep the societal sharing system intact and functional to serve the daily human needs for goods and services.

The divine gives us the choice. He recognizes us as "choice makers." Can we find fault with such conditionality? The choice-making foundation should be obvious as it resides in human uniqueness. Every human is unique in the universe. It is this uniqueness that manifests in different languages we speak. It is this uniqueness that determines how we choose to build our house and make our food. Everything among humankind comes as a mix of alternatives that have their origin at human uniqueness. Every aspect of human life is a composite of different choices that unique humans make. There is nothing in humankind done the same by all humans. We should not need a divine being to tell us this fact of human life, but apparently we do.

We often fail to see the human as "choice maker." History is full of instances where we kill each other in order destroy someone else's way, someone else's choice-making. The divine clearly recognizes that even a piece of divine knowledge cannot be uniformly accepted by all. There will be those that align themselves with the divine teaching and those that would want nothing to do with it and seek other alternatives. Such outcome reflects the inherent uniqueness of the human individual. We might be blind to human uniqueness in every aspect of life but we must at least see the uniqueness that comes in a variety of "sacred texts" given to us from divine sources throughout human history.

I have already noted that the Greek word translated "blessed" can equally be translated as "happy."[9] Whether translated blessed or happy it carries conditionality. One can be aware of poor knowledge giving or choose not to. One can be a fulltime knowledge seeker or stop after sixth grade. One can share with others everything one knows or share little and hide a lot. One can excel in knowledge giving or choose to give none. From the divine point of view such behaviors are human choices. In the Sermon on the Mount, the divine forces no one to become a knowledge giver. The divine only says that those who become aware of the "knowledge deficiency" associated with poor knowledge giving, and then counter it as knowledge seekers and knowledge sharers, would be "happy" in life.

Looking at the second beatitude

Starting from the first beatitude's knowledge seeking and knowledge sharing we arrive at the second beatitude where the divine asks if we can "mourn." The traditional view sees mourning as an aspect of the poor, but mourning is not an attribute of the poor. Instead, mourning signals a human stuck in very bad situations created by very low levels of knowledge giving. The second beatitude is asking if we as humans can relate to "very bad situations of knowledge giving" that appear in human life. The divine tells us that we will be happy if capable of recognizing the very bad knowledge-giving situations—the mourning situations.

Starting with the first beatitude's awareness of knowing that we are poor in knowledge giving, what would a knowledge seeker and knowledge sharer do when recognizing a mourning situation? To me the answer is obvious. All of the shared knowledge and resources and all knowledge seeking and knowledge giving would be directed to counter, remedy, address, and prevent the mourning situation. Or perhaps not. Similar to recognition of "knowledge-giving deficiency" the "recognition of mourning situations" is conditional. The divine knows the human to be always and under all conditions a "choice maker." One can be right in front of the humans suffering from a mourning situation and see nothing of significance and relevance. Such human is either incapable of mourning or chooses not to mourn and walk away. None of that choice maker's knowledge and capabilities are directed at addressing that mourning situation. Is something wrong with that kind of behavior? The divine does not see anything wrong with that behavior. All the divine says is that the choice maker would be happier if he or she can mourn and address the mourning situation through knowledge giving.

Who can possibly follow the first two?

The illusion that no one on earth is already following the instructions given in the Sermon on the Mount is ever present.

More specifically, with regard to what we have covered so far, there is the erroneous notion that no one would choose to follow the way of life spelled out in the first two beatitudes. How can I be so sure of my position? As evidence, all I need to do is to look at businesses set up all over the world. A large majority, if not all, have no awareness of what the divine says in the Sermon on the Mount, yet they all act according to what it says. How could that be possible? How could every business in the world whether in a Christian, Islamic, Buddhist, Hindu, or Confucian society act according to the divine recommendations in the first and second beatitudes? It is most easy to demonstrate that such is the case.

Just consider what you know about any business, regardless of how large or small it might be, and the products and services it produces and distributes. Every business in the world exists as knowledge seeker and knowledge sharer. It constantly seeks to obtain the knowledge it needs to produce and distribute goods and services and constantly acts as "knowledge giver" as each of its products and services is a "knowledge-packet" given to others. It is, however, constantly aware of the fact that it is "poor in knowledge giving," that its products and services come with defects, and it must constantly seek knowledge in order to address those never-ending defects and deficiencies.

Every business in the world is thus aligned with the first beatitude. I agree that the alignment is not perfect nor complete because the business and its employees and customers lack the direct awareness of what is said in the first beatitude. But even lacking that awareness, how can they be so aligned with the divine instructions? The answer is simple. The divine is telling us about the foundation of human life. Even when not knowing it, we cannot escape the foundation. This is like not knowing about the oxygen we breathe in the atmosphere yet nevertheless continuing to breathe it given it is a foundational aspect of life without which we cannot exist. Such is the case with the first beatitude. Regardless of our religious orientation, and regardless of our choice making tendencies, we naturally tend to align with what the divine is telling us in the first beatitude.

I might have sold you on the business world's alignment with the first beatitude, awareness of being poor in knowledge giving, but to what extent would the business world align itself with the second beatitude? The answer: by quite a bit. It may come as a total surprise that the supply and demand curves of all businesses are tools of "mourning management." I know I would be seriously mourning if I did not have food to eat, a bed to sleep in, or pharmaceuticals to lessen my ills. The business world is dedicated to constantly ensuring that no such mourning possibilities come to exist. Wherever and whenever there is the possibility that the lack of goods and services would give rise to a mourning situation, businesses recognize that possibility as "demand" and provide the goods and services that prevent the mourning situation. Similarly, if some goods and services are deficient, adversely affecting the human life leading to a mourning situation, the business world is quick to return to knowledge seeking and knowledge sharing to see what went wrong because of knowledge-giving deficiencies and address it so that such mourning situation does not occur again.

Recall, the alignment is not perfect nor complete. Mourning situations abound in many places in the world, but the reality is that without the businesses aligning themselves with the second beatitude the situation would have been much worse. The wonder of it all, such alignments are done everywhere on earth without any awareness of what the divine has said. What the divine says is a foundational aspect of human existence and manifests in human organization and activities regardless of whether the humans know it or not. Such foundational immersion is the case even when the method of mourning management is disguised in supply and demand terminology rather than the language of the Sermon on the Mount.

Arriving at the third beatitude

With this we arrive at the third beatitude where the divine tells us that we would be happy if we can be "meek." We started with being poor in knowledge giving and addressed it with knowledge seeking and knowledge sharing. We then recognized the significance of addressing the society's bad situations of knowledge giving—the mourning situations. How now are we to become the meek? What are we to do as "meek?" The traditional view sees the meek as an attribute of the "poor" and makes the third beatitude irrelevant for daily human life. But we are not traditional. Having started with knowledge giving, the main characteristics of the meek stand out as <u>patient</u> and <u>gentle</u>. The *patient* recognizes the role of time in human activity, does not rush, and seeks knowledge of alternatives before acting. The *gentle* does not use brute force on others regardless of what alternative is being pursued. From this perspective meek is the *nonviolent force manager and alternative-assessor*.

In the first two beatitudes we encountered poor knowledge giving and intensely bad knowledge giving. In the third beatitude we encounter "force management," "time," and "assessment of alternatives" as key factors when addressing knowledge-giving deficiencies. Time allows the development of alternatives and allows for knowledge seeking and knowledge sharing. If we rush, we can be deficient in knowledge seeking and knowledge sharing. If we rush, instead of addressing a knowledge deficiency we may only provide a bandage, leaving it to grow and repeat. If we rush with deficient knowledge, we almost always have to <u>force others</u> to share their capabilities in our chosen alternative and thus cannot be gentle.

Here we have to pause and wonder about the divine wisdom in how the beatitudes are ordered. Being meek does not come before awareness of knowledge-giving deficiencies. More significant, it does not come before the mourning situations. Why? The placement relative to the mourning situation is obvious. Removing the mourning situation is the only pressing alternative. If someone does not have food to eat today, we cannot patiently study the alternatives for the next three months. We must remove the mourning situation now, regardless of our level of knowledge, regardless of the knowledge deficiencies we face. We must immediately address the mourning situation with whatever knowledge we have at our disposal. Only in absence of the mourning situation can we behave in the manner of the meek. Similarly, before behaving in the manner of the meek, we have to be aware of being poor in knowledge giving. Such awareness is crucial to behaving as meek when searching for alternatives and avoiding the use of brute force in human interactions.

I have used the business world example to demonstrate the inherent alignment with the first and second beatitudes. Can I do the same with the third beatitude? The answer is "yes." To a large degree, the business world fits the meek behavior. It regularly assesses its alternatives for application of resources to production and distribution of goods and services. In general, it shuns violence within its borders and in the majority of its products and services. Again, the alignment is not perfect nor complete, yet there is substantial alignment even though practically no business is aware of what the divine is telling us in the Sermon on the Mount.

The fourth beatitude

In my other books I point out that every society has a "force-based resource taking" design. In all societies "justice," actual or ideal, refers to balancing the human interactions such that no one has to resort to brute force in order to satisfy one's needs and if anyone resorts to brute force it can be addressed so that the society and human interactions return to balance again. In the fourth beatitude, for the first time we see "justice" appearing in the divine teaching. It is the first time the divine points at balancing the force-based resource taking system. The divine knows that force never disappears from human life nor does the human behavior of resource taking to satisfy daily needs. The application of force and the taking of resources must be societally just—societally balanced.

In the third beatitude we encountered "force management"

and were told to use force gently. The gentle use of force always means the absence of brute force. In the fourth beatitude we are asked if we can be "righteous"—act in accordance with justice. Justice, regardless of how the society expresses it, is always about "management of differences and differentials among humans." It is about the management of uniqueness in how humans apply force and allocate resources. As human beings, everyone brings a different set of capabilities to the societal sharing system. How to manage the differences and differentials, an issue facing every society, is addressed in the fourth beatitude.

It is important to note that the divine does not tell us anything about what justice is or *how* we can manage justice. In short, the divine does not tell us how to set up and manage the force-based resource taking system. All that is left to human as choice maker. All that is left to us. All we are told is that we must, at all times and in all situations, remain utterly dedicated to maintaining the societal balance, the justice.

In the sequence of the beatitudes the divine teaches us another significant aspect of justice. Today every society starts with setting up a "force network" founded on brute force. Then, within that force network, the society sets up the resource taking processes that produce and distribute goods and services. Only then, after the societal force-based resource taking system is in place, humans engage in knowledge seeking and knowledge processing that seeks to maintain balance and achieve justice. This is the exact opposite of what the divine recommends in the beatitudes. Of course, a society that manages its knowledge-giving poorly, does not address its mourning situations, and cannot assess its alternatives patiently and nonviolently, will not be able to achieve justice in managing the differences and differentials among humans. That is why justice is not the first item among the beatitudes. The divine message is clear. We cannot manage justice well or reach societal balance if the starting point is brute force.

For thousands of years the Sermon on the Mount and more specifically the first four beatitudes have been deemed irrelevant to human life. They have failed to enter the societal sharing system to influence its design, even though as I have indicated, no society on earth can isolate itself from the divinely provided foundation of life that is the beatitudes.

As a professor, I regularly use the "water bottle example" in my classes, asking students how many humans are involved in the sharing processes that create one bottled water. I ask, what is the number of humans whose capabilities contribute to the creation of the bottled water? Initially my students estimate a number between a few to a few hundred depending on one's view of the number of workers at the bottling plant and those at the grocery store stocking and selling the bottled water. At that I ask, "Who provides the bottling plant's machinery?" Clearly those that created the bottling plant's machinery have part of their capabilities flowing into the bottled water. With that question the sharing horizon opens up because the machinery is made of metal and thus uncounted humans in mining, metal processing, and manufacturing industries have part of their capabilities flowing into the bottled water.

To this view I can add many other kinds of sharing that contribute to creation of the bottled water. For example, the bottled water has to be transported in a truck from the plant to the grocery store. Thus, part of capabilities of humans in auto manufacturing flows into the bottled water. The truck cannot deliver the bottled water to the grocery store without fuel, thus the whole oil industry, the refineries and gas stations, share in capabilities that flow to the bottled water. The truck could not function without roads and thus the capabilities of road builders and constructors flow into the bottled water. The bottling plant cannot operate without electricity and natural gas, thus part of the capabilities of all those in electric power plants, transmission and distribution lines, and natural gas pipelines flow into the bottled water.

All people I have identified so far with their capabilities flowing into the bottled water have to be fed if they are to be capable of sharing, so part of the capabilities of all farmers and ranchers flow into the bottled water. Then, all have to be sheltered, educated, and taken care of when sick, thus part of the capabilities of doctors, homebuilders, schools, and every other group performing similar tasks flows into the bottled water. Given the number of imports into the country, such sharing is not limited to the region and nation as much of the world supports some aspect of the life of the workers that share in creation of the bottled water. In short, the bottled water reaches the lone individual because of a "societal and perhaps global sharing arrangement" that has the capabilities of millions of humans flowing into one bottle of water to be used by one individual. This sharing condition is not unique to bottled water. You can start with anything that humans make and use, be it a pencil, a car, a computer, or even a "thought," and the answer is the same. Everything humans make and use sits at the crossroads of a huge sharing system that connects the shared capabilities of all to the goods and services that humans make and use in daily life.

And the surprising part? All "capabilities" are different forms of "knowledge giving." All capabilities originate in knowledge seeking and knowledge sharing. There is no exception. The societal sharing system is a "societal capability-sharing system." It is a "societal knowledge-giving system." Is this why it is so important to be aware of knowledge-giving deficiencies? Since all deficiencies flow and aggregate to become the human life as the "societal sharing system?"

Am I the only one to notice the societal sharing system? No. Others have noted it and most have walked away as if not a big deal. One such example comes from Adam Smith around two hundred years ago, describing the typical worker—the sharer of capabilities in the societal sharing system:

> Every part of his cloathing, utensils, and food has been produced by the joint labour of an infinite number of hands.[10]

In this description of the societal sharing system, Adam Smith uses the terminology of "joint labour" instead of "shared capabilities." In place of "millions" as used by me, Smith uses the phrase "infinite number of hands." Regardless, the point is the same. In every good and service made and used by humans, every human is linked to capabilities shared by uncounted millions of others. The infinite number of hands are infinite acts of knowledge giving that flow and aggregate to create life. It is this complex of societal and global sharing that produces and distributes goods and services for all and in doing so defines everyone's life. Its deficiencies are the deficiencies in human life.

Why am I telling you this story? It might even be a repeat, as I am sure I wrote similar things in my other books. The reason I am repeating is to see if in listening to the story you thought of the most important "sharer" in the societal sharing system, namely the divine. Did you notice that the divine is also a provider of capabilities into the societal sharing system? I doubt you did, but now you know. Imagine what happens to bottled water production if we decide we don't need food producers. How many bottles of water would be made if no one has food to eat? What if we make our decision a bit less harsh and produce food at the level of one meal per day and nothing more? This is deficient knowledge processing as we lack the knowledge that humans need three meals per day. How many bottles of water would be produced when everyone gets only one meal per day? A lot less and perhaps none. Today we see such examples in poor societies. They lack knowledge processing capabilities. They lack sharing possibilities in many dimensions and as such they are incapable of making and using many of the goods and services they need in daily life. They have no automobile manufacturing facilities, have constructed few roads, and a bottled water plant is irrelevant and out of reach.

Why am I drawing this dire picture? To make you aware that failing to fully take into account the knowledge shared by the divine is no different than failing to recognize that you need to have food production and sharing before you can have bottled water production and sharing. In every society, many of our problems originate at not fully incorporating the divine knowledge into our societal sharing system. Top of the list of the currently dismissed divine knowledge is the Sermon on the Mount.

II

A Side Glance at Opposition

It is important to understand the Sermon on the Mount teaching. It is equally important to know why it has remained obscure. The obscurity happens within the context of the religion organization, or more specifically, the "religion business" that has acted as the vehicle containing and transporting the Sermon on the Mount to future generations. What do we know about the religion business within which the Sermon on the Mount resides?

In one of my books I distinguish between what the divine tells us directly, like in the Sermon on the Mount, and when St. Paul says what the divine has said, like the stories told in the Gospels. I show that while St. Paul is a great figure in human history, his focus remains on promoting his religion business and not the divine knowledge given in the Sermon on the Mount. The difference between those two positions is immense. Yet we must be grateful to St. Paul's religion business as it is through his business activities that the Sermon on the Mount has been preserved for future generations like us.

Another drawback of St. Paul's religion business is its focus on serving the Greek market. As such, we do not have the divine words in the original language made available to humankind. All we have is the Greek translation of what the divine said. Even today, there is no way of knowing to what extent the English translation of the Greek version reflects the original divine words and to what extent it has been modified by the gospel writers that served the needs of St. Paul's religion business for operational documents. My assumption will be that the translations of the beatitudes accurately reflect the original divine words. My assumption lies in the concise and compact nature of this knowledge. It leaves little room for the translators to mess it up.

As a divine piece of knowledge, the Sermon on the Mount has always been problematic for the religion business. "Universality" poses the first thorny problem. The Sermon on the Mount is applicable to anyone regardless of belief. There is no prerequisite for anyone following it as a path of life. From the very moment of its arrival, the Sermon on the Mount's universal focus contrasts the Pauline religion business built around the doctrine of grace that dismisses the role and relevance of human capabilities in achieving a full life. Even when adding the religion business's claim that the Sermon on the Mount was written for those who had already received salvation by grace, it does not reduce the tension between the Sermon on the Mount and the Pauline tradition.

While I admire St. Paul as a hero of humankind, I need to be clear about my own tendency. I consider St. Paul and his words irrelevant in comparison with the divine words in the Sermon on the Mount. But I am alone. All those who are somebody in St. Paul's religion business take the opposite view. The words of St. Paul, the founding CEO of the religion business, reign supreme. For example, people like Augustine and Chrysostom, top executives in St. Paul's religion business, have persisted with declaring St. Paul's message as the foundation on which the Sermon on the Mount was built. Similarly, Martin Luther in his commentary on the Sermon on the Mount succinctly summarizes the dismissal of the divine when compared to St. Paul's teaching. The divine is talked about as a person that cannot distinguish between grace and merit. What the divine has expressed is dismissed as if a mistaken or erroneous view compared to what St. Paul has said. Here is an example of what Luther says:

> In this sermon we have heard Christ emphasizing works very rigorously. ... From these statements those silly false preachers have drawn the conclusion that we enter the kingdom of heaven and are saved by our own works and actions
>
> ...
>
> It is necessary that everyone should know at least a little about the distinction between grace and merit, for the two are mutually exclusive.[11]

Luther is also very clear as to the inferiority of the Sermon on the Mount, even though from every perspective it is the closest thing we have to the word of God:

> It is beyond understanding how through his apostles the wicked devil has managed so cleverly to twist and pervert especially the fifth chapter, making it teach the exact opposite of what it means. ... Still the infernal Satan has not found a single text in the Scriptures that he has more shamefully distorted and into which he has imported more error and false teaching than this very one, which Christ Himself ordered and appointed in order to head off false doctrine.[12]

There is no recognition by Luther that perhaps those like him and even St. Paul have not understood the word of God in the Sermon on the Mount. In fact the understanding of the word of God is not the issue at all. Luther's key point is this: as a divine document, the Sermon on the Mount renounces St. Paul's doctrine of grace and therefore must be put down not at as divine words but as works of Satan. On the surface Luther's comparative ranking is possible if the divine is just another Mediterranean Jew like St. Paul and divinity a fabricated facade.

I find it easier to explain this phenomenon in business terms. Placing St. Paul's words higher than those of the divine becomes a "business strategy," a behavior quite dominant even today. Outside religious organizations there is not a single business today that does not place the words of its CEO above the word of God. Within religion business the same pattern persists with only one difference. Religion business pays lip service to God while placing the CEO of the organization—St. Paul and the managers that followed him—above what the divine says because what the divine says lacks the market significance that the CEO's words carry for the organization. From the religion business point of view, St. Paul's words captured customers in the Greek market that the divine words in the Sermon on the Mount could not. This is the pattern that has persisted for over two thousand years and remains dominant over the divine knowledge in the Sermon on the Mount.

Starting with the marketing aspects, from the religion business point of view the Sermon on the Mount is not an "easy product" to sell and it cannot be readily adopted and used by consumers of religious products. This is especially the case when the religion business has no understanding of what the divine is saying and how it relates to key aspects of life like knowledge management and the earth transitioning between its two versions. Thus, the Sermon on the Mount would not be the type of product attractive to people considering St. Paul's organization for religious products. However, in contrast, the "grace theology" is the easiest and most attractive religious product one can get. All one needs to do is to believe and one gets the whole salvation package through grace. No extra work needs to be done. It is premade, prefabricated, and ready to use; just add "belief" which the human can easily do. This makes "grace" a highly attractive product not only for St.

Paul's organization but for any successful marketing program given, as still holds true today, "grace" is the easiest product a human can use. It demands nothing outside the individual's few-agree, personal "belief" and in return gives everything the human desires from a divine source.

As business strategy I understand why St. Paul's words are deemed superior to the divine words. But I have no interest in St. Paul's business strategy. What I am most interested in is understanding the Sermon on the Mount's universal message. Why? Because what St. Paul says does nothing for humans preparing to deal with the transition from blue-skied to canopied earth. Only what the divine says in the Sermon on the Mount matters.

Although St. Paul's religion business is totally opposed to the Sermon on the Mount, it cannot totally ignore it. It has to note that the beatitudes comprise a distinct, self-contained and compact section of the Sermon on the Mount. They are statements that have the authority of the divine behind them, intended to be learned by heart and remembered.[13] As to the order and arrangement of the beatitudes, the common tradition observes that:

> This arrangement is the result of literary design, rather than the accidental outcome of embellishment or expansion. What, then, are the reasons for this design, and what are its intentions?[14]

The religion business is keen on rejecting the Sermon on the Mount and to do so at its foundation, the first beatitude. To St. Paul's religion business the first beatitude has always been the center of interest, continually interpreted as something associated with "poverty" and the poor. How could such interpretation destroy the Sermon on the Mount? Why would the religion business see this approach as not promoting the Sermon on the Mount? Because if the Sermon on the Mount, the most systematic teaching of a divine being is about "the poor," then it is practically useless to the majority of humans. Why? Because every society is founded and maintained by the non-poor, those that successfully develop and share their capabilities with others. The "poor," by definition, are humans lacking in capabilities, deficient in sharing with others whatever capabilities they might have. No society on earth has ever been organized and maintained by the poor. The human societies exist on "shared capabilities" of the non-poor.

Regardless of the explanation we might choose for the first beatitude, one thing is clear. If it is about "the poor," it is a useless piece of knowledge. What every society needs is the foundational knowledge for capability sharing, not knowledge pertaining to a small and operationally irrelevant group that does not or cannot "share capabilities" well at this time.

So far I have portrayed the religion business as "opposition." I have talked about the two-thousand-year-old pattern of opposition and have given specific examples like Luther. But is it possible that the religion business's current view has changed, that today top executives of religion business think of the Sermon on the Mount differently? That is a fair question, so let me share the recent views of Pope Benedict about the Sermon on the Mount. Regarding the Pope, I can validly assume I am dealing with a person most familiar with the Sermon on the Mount. With that, how do we expect the Pope to treat the Sermon on the Mount? Clearly, in my line of reasoning, I am placing the Pope in the opposition group, the current CEO of St. Paul's religion business. If so, the key question would be one of how careful the Pope would be in declaring the Sermon on the Mount irrelevant to daily human life. Here is how it goes.

The Pope starts by implying that in the beatitudes the verse order is not correct. That to make sense of what the divine is saying, certain verses should be moved forward, others back. This is a subtle way of dismantling what the divine is teaching. Thus, the Pope starts with the first beatitude and then says:

> Let us pass over for the time being the second Beatitude listed in Matthew's Gospel and go directly to the third, which is closely connected with the first.[15]

I bet in this simple sentence you missed the Pope's subtle yet viscous destruction of the divine teaching in the Sermon on the Mount. No, it is not jumping from the first beatitude to the third. The ruinous rejection is to declare the divine instructions as a "list" in Matthew's Gospel. It is a list that Matthew has given, and with it you can do whatever you wish. The first thing that Pope Benedict does is to declare that in the beatitudes we are dealing with a human-made, "Matthew-made" list and that the order in the list is incorrect.

After going to the third beatitude, the Pope jumps back to the second beatitude and from there to the eighth beatitude. Here is what he says:

> Let us go back to the second Beatitude.[16]
> The second Beatitude is thus intimately connected
> with the eighth.[17]

From what I have told you in this book's first chapter, the verse order in the beatitudes is critical to what the divine is telling us. If we jump from "poor in knowledge giving" to "being meek and gently assessing alternatives" we are ignoring the mourning situations and as a result will not be able to gently assess alternatives as human life would be falling apart all around us. But the Pope is right in his intent: if you want to ignore the divine teaching in the Sermon on the Mount, say that it is a list put together by Matthew and since Matthew is just a human, it is easy to claim that his list is wrong, thus rejecting the list altogether.

The Sermon on the Mount's threat to the religion business is so strong that the Pope cannot end his opposition only at declaring the verse order being incorrect. He has to do more and does in the following way:

> The Beatitudes have to be read first and foremost
> in the context of the Bible.[18]

While I say the Sermon on the Mount and especially the beatitudes is standalone, complete and needs nothing else, the

Pope says it has no meaning outside the context of the Bible. This conveys whatever meaning is to be assigned to the Sermon on the Mount, it has to be within the operational context of the religion business that has the Pope as its CEO. He essentially declares that there is no "meaning" in the Sermon on the Mount and if we want to find meaning, we have to go to other sources. Thus he brings in other sources and declares them as giver of meaning to the Sermon on the Mount.

> The third Beatitude is practically a Psalm citation: "The meek shall possess the land" (Ps 37:11). ... In Numbers 12:3 we read: "Now the man Moses was very meek, more than all men that were on the face of the earth." One cannot help thinking of Jesus' saying, "Take my yoke upon you, and learn from me; for I am meek and lowly in heart" (Mt 11:29)[19]

The diversions and distractions come from what St. Paul's religion business claims the divine has said in various parts of the Gospels. Thus Pope Benedict concludes:

> Within the wide arc of these texts—from Numbers 12 through Zechariah 9 to the Beatitudes and the account of Psalm Sunday—we can discern the vision of Jesus, the king of peace.[20]

This is respectful dismantling of the Sermon on the Mount, a form of deferential opposition. The Sermon on the Mount has been dismantled and made conditional on all other stuff that the religion business offers as its goods and services. Done? No. If you said "done" you missed the degree of the threat that the Sermon on the Mount poses to the religion business. The Pope cannot stop there. He has to look for every other avenue of undermining the Sermon on the Mount and he does so first by inviting us to listen and value the advice of a rabbi who claims he would have rejected Jesus and the Sermon on the Mount if he were present

when Jesus was teaching it. Here is how the Pope describes the
rabbi's position:

> I have been greatly helped by the book I mentioned
> earlier by the Jewish scholar Jacob Neusner: *A Rabbi
> Talks with The divine.*
>
> …
>
> In this book, he takes his place among the crowds of
> Jesus' disciples on the 'mount' in Galilee. He listens
> to Jesus and compares his words with those of the
> Old Testament and with the rabbinic traditions
> as set down in the Mishnah and Talmud. He sees
> in these works an oral tradition going back to the
> beginnings, which gives him the key to interpreting
> Torah. He listens, he compares, and he speaks with
> Jesus himself. He is touched by the greatness and
> the purity of what is said, and yet at the same time
> he is troubled by the ultimate incompatibility that
> he finds at the heart of the Sermon on the Mount.[21]

Using a rabbi to beat on the Sermon on the Mount might be
powerful but in the eyes of the Pope, not sufficient. The Pope
needs to inflict more destruction on the Sermon on the Mount.
Thus, in conclusion, the Pope introduces the German philosopher,
Nietzsche, who has declared not only the Sermon on the Mount,
but Christianity as religion of slaves, irrelevant to the life of the
normal human. Thus the Pope remarks:

> But now the fundamental question arises: Is the
> direction the Lord shows us in the Beatitudes and
> in the corresponding warnings actually the right
> one? Is it really a bad thing to be rich, to eat one's
> fill, to laugh, to be praised? Friedrich Nietzsche
> trained his angry critique precisely on this aspect of
> Christianity. It is not Christian doctrine that needs
> to be critiqued, he says, it is Christian morality

that needs to be exposed as a 'capital crime against
life.' And by 'Christian morality,' Nietzsche means
precisely the direction indicated by the Sermon on
the Mount.[22]

With that the Sermon on the Mount gets torn apart, dragged
through every possible filth. Would anyone be able to recognize
the divine knowledge in the Sermon on the Mount after what the
Pope has chosen to do with it?

I am going to stop here and test you. I have already told you that
such is the style of the divine. Teach and test. He tells you about
the beatitudes and then tests you to see if you have understood
what he has taught. I'll talk about the specifics of the divine test in
a later chapter. For now it is my test on what you have read about
Pope Benedict, Rabbi Jacob Neusner, and Friedrich Nietzsche.

The test: what is the key aspect that the Pope, Neusner, and
Nietzsche have totally missed in their study and rejection of the
Sermon on the Mount?

One can say that they have missed the unity and universality
of the Sermon on the Mount. Even though that is important, it is
not the key. The key aspect that all three men have totally missed
is that the Sermon on the Mount is a "choice." The divine has no
problem with Pope, Neusner, and Nietzsche dismissing and not
using the Sermon on the Mount. The "choice" is the highlight
of every verse in beatitudes. Some will choose not to pay any
attention to the Sermon on the Mount and that is quite fine. All
the divine says to humans as choice makers is that they would be
"happy" if they made use of the divine knowledge given to them.
I fall into the category of people that choose to use the Sermon
on the Mount in their life while Pope Benedict, Neusner, and
Nietzsche fall into the category of people that choose not to use the
Sermon on the Mount in their life based on their own reasoning.
All that behavior is already known and incorporated into the
Sermon on the Mount.

Let me look at the Pope from a different angle. There are two
sides to what Pope Benedict is telling us about the Sermon on the

Mount. On the first side, he is the CEO of a religion business that for two thousand years has been most threatened by the Sermon on the Mount. That we understand. Every CEO in the world, in any time, would do the same. Whatever threatens the organization has to be destroyed or at minimum weakened and undermined. And he has done that like all previous CEOs of the religion business.

That was the first side, but the second side is more important. Pope Benedict readily falls into the group of "good humans." He is a good human. How can he be so wrong about the Sermon on the Mount? Or, is it possible that he is not wrong, that the Sermon on the Mount, as the Pope's argument purports, is nothing but garbage and it is I who is wrong? In theory, compared to Pope Benedict, I am a nobody. How can a nobody understand the Sermon on the Mount better than the Pope? The answer is easy. I might be the only human on earth that has been listening to "divine whispers" about the Sermon on the Mount. Everyone else has not heard the whispers or heard them and ignored them. In contrast, for forty years, I have been intently listening to these rare and occasional nudges directed at the humankind. In part, it is my connection to the divine whispers that makes my view of the Sermon on the Mount right and that of the Pope wrong. In part, it is forty years of nontraditional knowledge seeking and knowledge sharing compared to the Pope and the religion business that have only maintained and propagated their traditional two-thousand-year-old position.

How long have the divine whispers been flowing? Past 40 years, past thousand years, past 2000 years, or thousands of years before that? I don't know. All I know is that they have been flowing in my lifetime. To the typical human and definitely the typical scientist the notion of divine whispers sounds like total nonsense as I have no way of proving it, no way of recording it to say, "Aha, here it is, listen." The relevant thing to all humans is not the whispers I have received, but what I have put together with research and hard work after receiving the divine whispers. It is what I say in my books that should count.

III

The First Step the Tough One

I am always amazed at the way the human knowledge expands when a drop of divine knowledge gets added to it. I did not even add a drop of divine knowledge, all I added was a whisper or two. In my experience the divine whisper comes as the subtlest of an instant nudge—the still small voice. It is there for a fraction of a second and then there is nothing. You catch it at that instant or it is gone. That same whisper never repeats. It is through the divine whispers that I have learned the starting point. That is how I learned where the divine has placed the main piece of knowledge in the Sermon on the Mount—where it is tested and then practiced through case studies. While it is no longer a surprise to me, it might come as a surprise to you that the main divine knowledge is given to us in eight verses in the beatitudes. The traditional view sees the beatitudes as the main divine knowledge. It sees the first beatitude as the base, the others built on it. I agree with that.

What does the human get if one mixes the beatitudes into one's knowledge base when setting one's way of life? In each beatitude the outcome is specified. The outcome common to all beatitudes is the word that in the religious tradition is translated "blessed." The translation could have equally been "happy." I like "happy" better because it is human-centered. If I become happy, I am the one that is happy. I am the one that creates the condition of "happy." I don't like the word "blessed" as it points to an outsider that does the blessing. It undermines the divine teaching that the human is the "choice maker." It is the human that makes the choice of following the beatitudes and it is the human that would experience the outcomes of such choice. The word "blessed" brings in an outsider, often the religion business's rituals, that give the human the blessing. That is counter to what the divine teaches in every beatitude, namely the human as choice maker.

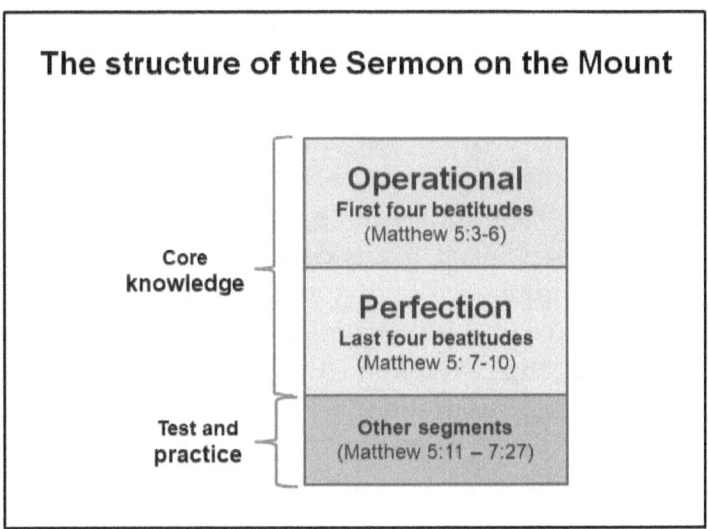

In the Sermon on the Mount, therefore, the main divine knowledge is in the beatitudes. Everything else is to prepare us, to test our understanding, and to make us practice the application of beatitudes to daily human life. The first four beatitudes are about the operational aspects of life, defining the core knowledge we need in our way of life. After humans have become good at using and applying them to their daily life, the second four beatitudes come into play as a method of perfecting the first four beatitudes. Thus, at the start, we do not need to focus on anything but the first four beatitudes. It is like going to the grade school of life and only after completing it can we think about the high school of perfection.

Before losing sight of it, let me point out that only a divine being is capable of expressing the full human life in just four brief verses. No human can do so. It is beyond the human capabilities. Moreover, only a divine being can recognize all this as human choice, see all knowledge processing originating from human choice. If the beatitudes were a human creation, or more specifically the product of a religion business, they would be full of must and should and never allow the possibility of choice making. That is also why for two thousand years the religion business has been adamant at undermining and dismissing the Sermon on the Mount. Okay, I have told you what I might have forgotten to say. Let me get back to the first beatitude.

The traditional view correctly recognizes the division of the eight beatitudes into two four-verse units. It also recognizes that the first beatitude is the foundational component on which all others rest. But from that point on, it only develops the misunderstanding of what the beatitudes are saying and then gets completely lost. What is the source of the problem? According to the traditional view it is "the strange expression 'the poor in (the) spirit'—if this is its proper English translation."[23] The first beatitude teaches us:

> [5:3] Blessed are the poor in spirit: for theirs is the kingdom of heaven.[24]

The traditional view is stuck in the first beatitude because it claims it does not know what the "poor in spirit" means. Many explanations rely on words that hope, by chance, might hit the target. For example, does the word "poor" refer to:

Economic poverty, or is it used as a spiritualized metaphor signifying the meaning of 'mentally depressed,' 'fainthearted,' or 'conscious of a general state of deprivation?' Or does it refer to 'voluntary poverty'?[25]

From there the traditional view jumps to the word "spirit." Does it refer to human spirit or divine spirit? The much simpler notion that "poor in spirit" is pointing at deficiency in "spirit" escapes the traditional view. Why? Why does the two-thousand-year-old view have no interest in a meaning well known to them, namely spirit as "knowledge giver"? From what we have seen from Luther and Pope Benedict, the last thing the traditional view wants is to make the Sermon on the Mount the knowledge relevant to humankind. That is why in their search for meaning they constantly look where the meaning does not reside.

In the search for meaning the traditionalist is quick to remind us that the expression "poor in spirit" is found only in this verse of the New Testament and cannot be found elsewhere in all of Greek language and literature. Since even for Greeks it is difficult to understand this expression, and since it is about "spirit" which the traditional view does not want to see as "knowledge giver," then the traditional focus plays with the word "poor," often deciding that from there everything in the Sermon on the Mount is about the "poor humans" and poverty. To make the first beatitude about the poor and poverty is bad reasoning. Let me pause and ask, in what I just said, did you see something interesting? Did the words "bad reasoning" catch your eye from a completely different direction? Let me explain. Notice when I say "bad reasoning" it is the same as saying "poor in reasoning." This should be of interest to us because no one would accept that the expression "poor in reasoning" is about the "poor" and not about deficiencies in reasoning. The same simple pattern of knowledge processing applies to the "poor in spirit." It is not about the poor but about *deficiencies in the spirit* and that is why we need to understand what "spirit" means.

I am always intrigued at the level of effort that traditionalists apply to declare that such is not the case. They persist the sole focus of the divine is that of spiritualized poverty. Or more so, that the intention was to involve the human mind and consciousness in the problem of poverty as becoming aware of poverty is good for one's general understanding of life. At its best moment, the traditional view admits that the first beatitude "points to an *intellectual insight* into the human condition" and in the same breath declares that such insightful attitude is the same as "humility."[26] All such nonsensical explanations are thrown at us so that we would not consider the one relevant meaning that poor in spirit is the same as "being bad in knowledge giving"—to be bad in knowledge seeking, knowledge sharing, and knowledge processing. Such knowledge-based, knowledge-driven meaning would change the world; playing with the word "poor" does not.

In traditional reasoning the word "spirit" disappears from the dialogue. Everything gets focused on the word "poor." Buried in that mindset we are told that "wealth" is not to be trusted and instead living in poverty is the ideal way of life because that is how the gods live—gods live in happiness because they are in need of nothing. Thus the poor are godlike in their lack of needs.[27] Such logic is based on total bull, but in principle is no different than Pope Benedict declaring that the verse order in the beatitudes is incorrect, that their meaning can only be understood in terms of other Bible verses, or that rejection of the Sermon on the Mount by people like rabbi Neusner and philosopher Nietzsche invalidates it.

Besides seeing such behavior emanating from an utterly scared religion business, it is beyond me how a human can construct the moronic "wealth is bad and poor is good" model, and worse, promote it as essence of life. In such model there is no recognition of the fact that "wealth" is an outcome of capability sharing among humans in order to provide for the needs of all. In the courses I teach I tell students that "wealth" is a device that defines the success of the societal capability sharing in the following ways: First, **wealth is a measure of "efficiency" in capability sharing**. It relates the inputs and outputs of capability sharing. If the capability sharing cannot generate wealth it means the inputs are always larger than outputs and soon the capability sharing will run out of resources to sustain itself. Second, **wealth is a measure of "value" to people that need goods and services through capability sharing.** If I organize people to share their capabilities to produce goods and services and no one wants my goods and services, I will sell nothing and generate no wealth. It would signal that what I do has no "value" to other humans. Wealth signals that the others want and value the goods and services that a certain group of humans produce through shared capabilities. Third, **wealth is a measure of "amplification of capabilities."** If I have wealth of $10, my ability to organize the capabilities of others to produce goods and services will be zero. However, if I have wealth of $10 million, my ability to organize the capabilities of others increases immensely. The wealth-based amplification of capabilities exists at all levels, from individuals to workplaces to nations.

The efficient, value-driven, and capability-amplified wealth manifests itself visibly in the societal life. As example, in comparing the societal sharing system of the typical African society with the US, the US can produce and distribute goods and services at a level impossible in the African society because of the wealth the US has produced in its societal sharing system. The US amplifies its capabilities beyond what the typical African nation can. The efficiency and value that the US creates is beyond what the typical African nation does. Wealth is the key performance measure of the societal sharing system in providing for the daily needs of all.

The lesson is obvious. Lacking what one needs in daily life signals low levels of capability sharing among humans to provide for each other's needs. It is a serious condition that must be addressed and remedied rather than accepted and tolerated under the moronic claim that it makes us similar to gods in needing nothing. It never makes sense to assume that the fewer things we have and the greater we suffer in our inability to provide for our daily needs, the closer we get to the divine. Such illusion is most dangerous for humans as knowledge seeker and choice maker as it traps the human in low levels of knowledge processing and in conditions of utter pain and suffering attached to the suitcase word "poor." So, not only is there nothing wrong with wealth, it is critical to societal well-being and human existence. To the contrary, not having wealth and being "poor" is the worst that an individual or society could experience in life. Yet in its effort to discredit and dismiss the Sermon on the Mount, the religion business has embarked on selling the notion that being poor is a good thing. Nothing can be more moronic in human life.

At a point like this it is natural to think of "conspiracy." Have I discovered a two-thousand-year-old conspiracy dedicated to rejection of the Sermon on the Mount? I don't think the rejection has anything to do with conspiracy but everything with the survival needs of the religion business. Such behavior has existed for two thousand years and is so ingrained in the religion business's operation and structure that a good person like Pope Benedict cannot see anything but what the religion business has propagated for 2,000 years.

From what we have seen, if the first verse of the beatitudes is understood correctly it becomes impossible to reject the Sermon on the Mount. It becomes impossible to declare it irrelevant to daily human life. Yet the religion business perceives and justifies its own existence in the rejection of the Sermon on the Mount by making it something relevant to the poor and not to the majority of humans that create and maintain the societal sharing system. Even though I know the truth of the Sermon on the Mount and do so primarily through the divine whispers I have received, I wonder if what I know makes any difference in the way humans currently think and behave. The religion business is large and powerful. It has conditioned generations of humans to see the Sermon on the Mount as irrelevant to daily human life. Such intense generational conditioning may persist for thousands of years to come. If so, no one would listen to what I say. Nonetheless, when my thoughts fall into such domain of despair, all I hear is "the human is the choice maker and knowledge processor." At final count, our societal sharing system reflects what we have chosen. We get what we choose. How much divine knowledge we add to our societal sharing system is entirely a human choice.

Why focus on the business world?

When it comes to implementing the Sermon on the Mount, the best place in human societies is the workplace where capabilities are shared in order to serve the daily needs of all for goods and services. I have already mentioned the place that practices the beatitudes most is the workplace even though it is done without awareness of what the divine has said in the Sermon on the Mount. But there is another aspect of the workplace you also need to take into account: the workplaces collectively form the "business world" and on earth *every human* lives in the "business world." How can that be? How can every human reside entirely in the business world? Easy.

Every human applies capabilities within the workplace that businesses set up and manage. All those working in government do so based on resources the workplace transfers to government as taxes. We buy the goods and services we need for daily life at stores the business world sets up and operates. We live in the houses built by the business world, eat the food created by the business world, take the medicine prepared by the business world, sleep on the bed provided by the business world, and get educated by books published by the business world. In short, humans are born in the business world, live in it, and die in it. Almost one hundred percent of our time is spent in the business world. There is no exception. Everyone lives in the world of goods and services provided by the business world. Everything that the business world does encompasses "knowledge-packets," combinations of human knowledge and earth material.

The business world is deeply relevant and important to human life. The Sermon on the Mount is all about the business world, namely how humans create and process knowledge and share capabilities to produce goods and services for the daily needs of all humans. Everything the business world does is centered on the creation and distribution of "knowledge-packets" we know as goods and services. I repeat, all goods and services are knowledge-packets, combinations of human knowledge with earthly material.

At present, the business world is ignorant of the Sermon on the Mount and only the religion business argues—claims—that a prominent piece of divine knowledge delivered to humankind, namely the Sermon on the Mount, has nothing to do with the business world—or in other words, has nothing to do with daily human life. We already know that is a false claim.

The business world is the backbone of the societal sharing system. It creates and manages the societal sharing system. It must be maintained at all times if humans are to receive the goods and services they need in daily life. The divine teaching in the Sermon on the Mount is significant for the business world from the point of maintenance and sustaining the societal sharing system. Any potential danger facing the business world is a key threat to human life that must be seriously considered. The earth is going to undergo a radical change. It will not exist as we know it today. I have briefly talked about it in this book as canopied earth and have covered it in detail in my other books. If in the transition from blue-skied to canopied earth we do not manage the structure and operations of the business world well, the whole of humanity will be in deep trouble. If the mythical end-of-the-world expectations are to be trusted, without an intact and viable societal sharing system no one will survive and humankind will come to an end.

The traditional view places the total destruction of the business world under the heading of "eschatology," the end time when the earth as we know it ends and the time for a different version of the earth begins. The "eschaton" is the event that changes the earth. While those pushing the idea of eschaton cannot tell us the physics behind the event, we know the word eschaton is the same as the transition from the blue-skied to canopied earth. The word eschaton is meant to scare us, but that would be fear in face of ignorance. No such fear is present in the beatitudes where we are told we are to deal with eschaton as "kingdom of heaven" whose science we now know as canopied earth.

We should not approach life, and more specifically the business world, in a fear-based manner but seek a knowledge-based approach. Such behavior does not need the knowledge of the canopied earth expressed in the ignorance-based language of eschaton. Many known cases in human history have come close to destroying the business world such as world wars, and ultimately will do so if conducted using nuclear weapons. But for an illustrative example we do not need to use the familiar example of war. We can go to the situation of fifteen thousand years ago when a good chunk of planet earth, including most of the state in which I live, namely Ohio, was under mile-high ice sheets. Science knows a lot about the ice sheets and knows that sooner or later they are going to show up, but it knows of no recipe as to what to do when they arrive. It does not know how the human societies are to face the ice sheets and survive. Sadly, science has decided that in search of knowledge it not only has no need for the Sermon on the Mount but that any such knowledge is nothing but superstition and nonsense. There you have it, the science community passing judgment on divine knowledge. But the reality of ice sheets remains. Mile-high ice sheets are a version of the earth radically different from what we have today. How would we manage our lives if the ice sheets show up in full force a hundred years from now? What the divine in the Sermon on the Mount recommends is this: to manage the new earth's radical conditions well, humans are better off, aka more happy, applying their life according to the knowledge given in the Sermon on the Mount.

Note the ice sheet example comes from a radical change caused by natural and cosmic sources. But radical change can also be human-made. What about the radical change caused by excess CO_2 humans add to the atmosphere, causing the so-called global warming? (Assume substantial knowledge deficiencies in wrapping our heads around the concept of global warming.) What about something much simpler with much higher knowledge content as to its outcome of radical change? What about a global nuclear war? Assume some humans survive the nuclear war. What is the best way of living for the survivors of the global nuclear war? The answer: even in those direst of life conditions, the best chance for the small number of survivors living in a radically altered earth is to line up with the divine teaching in the Sermon on the Mount and follow the way spelled out in the beatitudes. That is the only way that they might resurrect a shadowy image of the business world that they so readily chose to destroy.

I know for a fact that so long as humans do not comprehend the significance of the Sermon on the Mount in their lives, they will remain incapable of understanding the significance of the business world and the societal sharing system in their life. They cannot see that life is based on shared capabilities and not on destroyed capabilities. Lacking the key component, the divine knowledge in their societal sharing system, they will continue to see wholesale destruction of the societal sharing system as something unavoidable.

Understanding and managing "knowledge deficiency"

When we start with "poor in spirit" and declare it means "deficiency in knowledge giving" and that the deficiency in knowledge giving demands humans engage in knowledge seeking and knowledge sharing, what do we mean by such activities? How can we make it clear what we mean by knowledge seeking and knowledge sharing? Let us start with the classroom, the simplest form of knowledge giving in human societies. What are its key components? Teacher and student. Who are they? Can we see the student as knowledge seeker and the teacher a representative of society's "knowledge sharers"?

Do we see the teacher as knowledge sharer feeding "shared knowledge" to students, the knowledge seekers? This all seems fine and good. The society has created a "knowledge base" from shared human capabilities and the purpose of the classroom is to introduce the students to this societally shared knowledge base. That way the students grow to become knowledge sharers that link their capabilities to the societal sharing system in order to produce goods and services for the needs of all. But there is a deficiency here, a deficiency in knowledge giving. Can you see it?

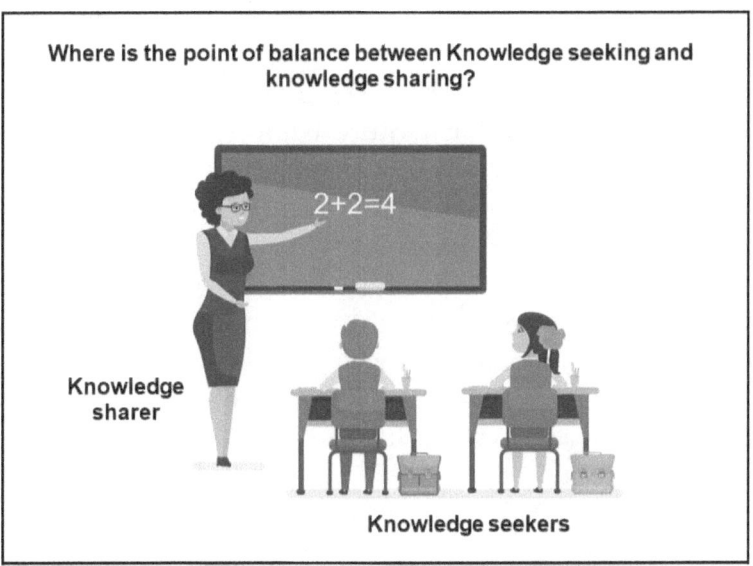

If a knowledge sharer dominates the scene, the individual student's knowledge base becomes only a container filled by the societal shared knowledge. There is little knowledge seeking that the individual student does on his or her own. This becomes especially true if the teacher teaches with a strong element of force to make students behave as if they are mechanical containers only to be filled with what the teacher knows. Under such circumstances the students grow to become adults that fill spots in the societal sharing system as managers and workers but remain low on "knowledge seeking" which makes them low on "knowledge giving." In such approach, as students or adults, humans would basically do what they have been taught to do. Nothing more. They are deficient, disconnected from the societal sharing system ideally defined as the network of shared capabilities of knowledge seekers.

Now consider the other extreme. The teacher fills the student with little to no societally shared knowledge and instead allows them to act as independent knowledge seekers, each developing their own view of the world based on their personal few-agree positions. In this way they grow to become knowledge seekers centered on their own world of few-agree positions paying little if any attention to the societal shared knowledge built around many-agree positions. They would behave awkwardly and incompetently if placed in positions that require using the societally shared knowledge to produce goods and services for others.

This is the dilemma humans face in the current way of addressing knowledge deficiencies. Lean too far toward the society's shared knowledge and one becomes incapable of expanding that knowledge base through knowledge seeking. Lean too far toward knowledge seeking and neglect the society's shared knowledge and you would create humans that excel in pursuing their own views and ways of life as the society built on sharing crumbles all around them.

So where is the point of balance? We do not know and have to figure it out. All we know is that our knowledge-giving deficiencies have to be addressed through a balanced mix of knowledge seeking and knowledge sharing. If we fail, we would end in many "mourning situations," either as a society stagnating in what it does, incapable of meeting the emerging and evolving needs of humans in daily life, or a society so dedicated to satisfying the individual needs that it readily collapses because it has little or no way of satisfying the daily needs of all through a system of societally shared capabilities.

Here is another key aspect when addressing knowledge-giving deficiencies. When we look at knowledge deficiencies we have to first recognize that "knowledge" always takes form within a matrix of force and resources. How the society manages force, structures its force network, and how it decides to produce and exchange goods and services using its resources define how knowledge takes shape and where it is deficient. The knowledge-giving deficiencies are thus embedded in force application deficiencies and resource allocation deficiencies. Managing force and resource deficiencies are inherent to taking care of knowledge-giving deficiencies.

Every knowledge-giving "deficiency" is like a broken or damaged link or connection in the societal sharing system. Knowledge deficiency is a "connection deficiency" among humans. It is the *connections* that create the societal sharing system and serve every individual. The more deficient humans become in knowledge giving, the fewer the connections they have and the weaker their societal sharing system becomes. Taking care of knowledge deficiencies is the only way of taking care of the societal sharing system to make it a viable arrangement for the lives of all.

Visiting the opposition as rejectionist

If we fall into the rejectionist trap and not see the "poor in spirit" as "knowledge-giving deficiency" but things like "poverty," then the whole Sermon on the Mount becomes irrelevant to human life. Persistence with knowledge-based understanding of the first beatitude avoids the two-thousand-year-old trap. We would no longer accept the traditional view that the expression "poor in spirit" means *poverty* and that somehow the divine knowledge was meant for the poor only, namely those not good in sharing capabilities—those that despite inabilities are either happy with their own miserable condition or are blessed for being miserable by some "agent of blessing," like the Church. This clearly is bad reasoning.

The human as capability sharer cannot glorify those that are bad in capability sharing—it is the capability sharer that needs to be glorified. To do so, especially to address those poor in developing and sharing capabilities, the human individual must know that everyone is deficient in "knowledge giving." To excel in capability sharing, to provide for the needs of all, the human must always move in the direction of addressing the knowledge-giving deficiencies. It is a movement toward a target the human can never quite reach but must always try to attain for the target is the condition where knowledge deficiencies do not exist, the condition of the divine. The human being created in the divine image seeks to become closest to the divine. That is the way of the human as knowledge seeker, knowledge sharer, and knowledge processor.

"Knowledge giving" is how humans seek and share knowledge in applying capabilities to provide goods and services for the needs of all. Everything that we buy and use as goods and services is the result of knowledge giving by others. It should be the most obvious evidence for the significance of knowledge giving in human life and the continual need to address the knowledge-giving deficiencies in every aspect of life. The knowledge-giving deficiencies always include deficiencies in application of force and allocation of resources. The deficiencies in knowledge giving are always deficiencies in "connection" to others. When connections to others are deficient—damaged or nonexistent, the entire societal sharing system becomes deficient and in the long-term harms everyone. The focus on knowledge-giving deficiencies is thus a foundational view of human life. A divine being has offered this foundational view to humans as knowledge processor and choice maker. The human can choose to follow the way of the first beatitude among various alternatives in life, or not. The divine allows the human to remain the choice maker. The human is created to be a choice maker.

In countering the rejectionist views we have learned that the first beatitude is not about poverty or humility but about human recognition of deficiencies in "knowledge giving." Recall knowledge-giving deficiencies always imply deficiencies in application of force and allocation of resources. What does that mean? For example, it means those that ignore or tolerate knowledge deficiencies and do not engage in knowledge seeking and knowledge sharing become targets. They become "resource taking opportunities" for those that engage in knowledge seeking and knowledge sharing in order to exploit the knowledge-deficient humans. The knowledge deficiency can and does function as the locus of temptation to organize for excessive resource taking.

But what if humans choose to follow the way of the first beatitude and constantly improve their knowledge position? High levels of knowledge sharing and knowledge seeking do not eliminate the human individual's tendency for resource taking but do eliminate excessive resource taking and moderate the resource taking levels in production and distribution of goods and services. In life, the knowledge-based approach provides a better structure for management of force and resources to satisfy the daily needs of humans for goods and services. Any excessive resource taking signals the presence of knowledge deficiencies that have not yet been addressed. It signals deficiencies in application of force and allocation of resources that likewise have not been addressed.

Force, resources, knowledge

Today's force-based societies allow the resource takers to "fight it out" and compete so that the level of resource taking can be lowered through competition. But many such fighters soon learn that "collusion" or "follow the leader" is a better strategy than direct competition if they are to sustain high levels of resource taking. Thus the force-based societies always regress into high levels of resource taking. I have already indicated that excessive resource taking signals deficiencies in societal management of knowledge, force, and resources.

How do force management deficiencies manifest in excessive resource taking? The problem with excessive resource taking is that it always invites direct use of brute force to counter it. Either the human individual that does not do well in resource taking has to resort to brute force, or the society has to design its force network to counter the possibilities for excessive, colluded resource taking. This in turn brings more "brute force" into human life and expands the possibilities for destructive release of brute force.

Lowering the level of resource taking and eliminating the possibilities for excessive resource taking are not compatible with the force-based way of life. The force-based system will eventually spiral out of control and in the process destroy the society. The same type of argument will apply to knowledge deficiencies that manifest as resource allocation deficiencies. The resource allocation deficiencies always feed into force management deficiencies. The knowledge-based way of the Sermon on the

Mount, however, allows the society to move away from the force-based focus and instead organize itself in the knowledge-based way that continually addresses the knowledge deficiencies in human life and lowers the level of exposure to brute force and mournful resource allocations.

IV

Deeper into the Second Step

We now know that the first beatitude focuses on knowledge-giving deficiencies. With that we arrive at the second beatitude which says:

> 5:4 Blessed are they that mourn: for they shall be comforted.

The second beatitude's "Can you mourn?" is simply asking if we are capable of recognizing and addressing really bad deficiencies in knowledge giving. For the human practicing the first beatitude, namely being aware of and identifying knowledge-giving deficiencies, the second beatitude focuses on whether the practitioner of the first beatitude can see the "mourning situations," situations where the knowledge-giving deficiencies are really bad. Understanding the second beatitude becomes that simple once we understand the first beatitude. So let us make it more difficult by asking how the traditional opposition—the rejectionists—have approached the second beatitude.

The traditionalist view relies on bad reasoning to erect walls of ignorance around every piece of the Sermon on the Mount in order to reject it. To the traditional view the second beatitude can only have two possible meanings. First, it is about specific losses like the death of loved ones. Second, it is about concepts like grieving over sinfulness. Nowhere in the traditional view do we find "mourning" to mean "facing situations of pain and suffering in daily human life" because of "knowledge-giving deficiencies." No mention of mourning especially in relation to absence of goods and services one needs for daily life. Note that by "goods and services" I do not mean what we find in the grocery stores but every aspect of human life including what we find in schools, homes, hospitals, and any other place where capabilities are shared to serve the human needs.

Starting from the first beatitude it is easy to see that deficiency in knowledge giving is the source of all sorts of mourning, especially when the deficiency relates to the goods and services the human needs in daily life. From my own experience I know I would be mourning seriously if I did not have a house, car, computer, food, and pharmaceuticals. The second beatitude is asking, "Can you mourn?" It questions whether the human "can relate to situations of intense pain and suffering." The human that cannot relate to pain and suffering of self and others through observing the knowledge-giving deficiencies would be incapable of following the way of life the divine teaches.

It is possible that a person can be the greatest knowledge giver of all time but still fail to walk the way of the divine because of the inability to "mourn;" the inability to see the intense knowledge-giving deficiencies to which *other humans* are exposed. But if the human recognizes the pain and suffering of self and others in knowledge-giving deficiencies, then the focus would become one of addressing and removing such instances of pain and suffering.

"Mourning" indicates a situation of high knowledge deficiency. It also implies a situation of extreme deficiencies in application of force and allocation of resources. It signals conditions where there is little if any "connection" among humans and thus only an empty shell of the societal sharing system. How to address the mourning or how to stop it requires the improved flow of knowledge among many. Those who can mourn would recognize the knowledge deficiency that sits at the core of pain and suffering and would behave in ways to address it. They would point at force management deficiencies and resource allocation deficiencies within whose matrix the knowledge deficiencies reside.

What is unique to the beatitudes is that it makes *everyone* responsible for deficiencies in knowledge seeking, knowledge sharing, and most importantly, knowledge giving. There is no hierarchical structure where bosses are made the responsible group and employees are left to themselves. Every human will be happy if focused on knowledge-giving deficiencies along all directions and especially the mourning situations that cause intense pain and suffering on humans.

The outcome of addressing the extreme situations of pain and suffering would be exactly as the divine has said. With removal of pain and suffering to self and others through management of knowledge-giving deficiencies, we would be happy and find comfort in life. Note that such removal of the mourning situations is not possible or would be incomplete if the human sees the force-based system as a way of life, or shuns the force-based system but remains unaware of "knowledge-giving deficiencies" as the foundational essence of human existence. Contrary to the divine teaching, the force-based way of life is quite at home with causing pain and suffering and finds sustaining the situations of mourning valuable, like bombing the cities of the humans labeled the "enemy."

In the force-based system, the appearance and maintenance of pain and suffering are not unique to what one society does to its enemies but also what it does to its own people. Not addressing the society's mourning situations invites "brute force explosions." The brute force explosions happen in two ways. They happen occasionally in the form of riots, terrorism, and revolution. They also happen continuously as "application of brute force" on humans in the form of theft and murder. All such manifestations of brute force, without exception, disrupt the force network and in doing so make the society's production and distribution of goods and services dysfunctional. Riots, terrorism, theft, and murder all are signs of extreme knowledge-giving deficiencies not addressed.

The mourning situations are inherent to the force-based society. The traditional view seeks a reasoned view of their meaning. If in the first beatitude the general human condition is set as "poverty," the second beatitude sets the expected human response as "grief." Thus poverty and grief become inseparable twins and according to the traditionalists they reach their peak at the point of human response to death. Sounds like a simple and real model. The key to this model is that it exists at the extreme periphery of the human life and has nothing to do with the daily human life. Death is a tiny component of the human life. Much of human life is occupied with living. The death-focused model makes the divine teaching in the Sermon on the Mount irrelevant to the daily human life. The poverty-grief model makes itself robust by adding "death" as an evil presence in human life. Since the focus is not on "daily life," the only thing remains is death, the end point of life. Why do we "mourn" the dead, given that the dead are gone from life and no longer exist? The answer: the purpose of the poverty-grief model is not to mourn for the dead but to chain the living human to the fear of death. The model wants us to mourn our own "fear of death," and since we have to seek some form of coming to terms with such fear, the traditionalist is quick to point out that we can do so by directing attention to the vague idea of "afterlife."

My point here is not that death is not real or that the concept of afterlife lies outside of human interests, but that the divine teaching in the Sermon on the Mount is focused on things that the human does while living and acting on earth. For two thousand years the traditionalist has thrown the divine out of human life and has transported the Sermon on the Mount teachings as far away from the daily human life as possible. This is in total contrast to the reality of the divine teaching that asks, "Are you capable of mourning? Are you capable of seeing pain and suffering of self and others? Are you capable of seeing the knowledge-giving deficiencies that cause such pain and suffering?" Only if we are capable of mourning can we focus on addressing the knowledge deficiencies that create intense situations of pain and suffering and act to remove them from the human life. Instead of accepting the death-focused poverty-grief model, it is through addressing knowledge deficiencies and removing pain and suffering that we make the human life the way it should be.

The traditional view states that "mourning is to be praised."[28] It completely misses the point that any praise of mourning would come from the ability to see and sense pain and suffering of self and others, then engage in knowledge processing to address and eliminate the corresponding knowledge-giving deficiencies. Here is the irony. The traditional view *does see* the obvious that:

> Mourning is the reaction to human deprivation and loss in all their forms.[29]

But instead of understanding the situation in terms of knowledge-giving deficiencies that must be addressed and removed when responding to deprivation and loss, it concludes that the reaction has to be one of:

> Not to deny but to accept the deplorable facts of human life.[30]

In short, the traditionalist view wants the human to stay with the death-based poverty-grief model and do nothing about it, even though to every human such position makes no sense.

Every human caught up in poverty is inherently a knowledge processor and choice maker. Every human facing situations of poverty and grief seeks to find ways of getting out and not staying in. The traditionalist interpretation says, stay in and take it like a man! The divine teaching says the exact opposite. The difference becomes most glaring when we add that what the divine is telling us has the canopied earth in mind. We are going to face the eschaton of the canopied earth, namely the transition from the blue-skied to canopied earth. That transition can put every unprepared human in a situation of celestial poverty. We will be facing a situation that no human alone can face and survive. In my books on the science of canopied earth, I mention that the beginning of the transition will not last more than a day, but comes with many possibilities for infliction of harm. For example, it could drop large comet fragments into the ocean and cause huge tsunamis. Those not following the divine and trapped in the death-based poverty-grief interpretation might sit, watch, and do nothing, or worse, resort to brute force and destroy everything that the tsunami does not. Only the correct understanding of the divine teaching will allow us to achieve the purpose of the divine teaching which is to prepare humans for eschaton's arrival. When following the divine we will be prepared for the transition as today we prepare to have lunch. We will be followers of the divine, capable of recognizing and addressing any mourning situation, current or future, through knowledge processing that takes care of the knowledge-giving deficiencies.

The most important aspect of the divine teaching about mourning situations is the "outsiders" looking into the mourning situation and not the person in pain and suffering looking out for help. In the force-based system, the person in pain and suffering has to be the originator of action to take care of the problem being faced. It is the suffering individual that must approach the outsiders. The divine teaching in the Sermon on the Mount reverses this process. It is not just the individual in pain and suffering but the masses of outsiders that are asked if they can mourn, and in being able to mourn, respond to knowledge-giving deficiencies that create extremes of pain and suffering. They are the ones that must identify and address the mourning situation. In today's force-based system, little gets directed toward the mourning situations and the person or groups in pain and suffering are largely left to themselves to address the situation. Most pointedly, this is not the case for the nations separated by oceans but people in the same city. Unaware of the second beatitude, unable to mourn, we cannot see the intense cases of pain and suffering directly staring us in the face, every day. The rich part of the city leaves the poor part of the city to itself; a wall of brute force separates the two and maintains the separation. The divine teaching reverses the mindset and extends it to the whole world. It asks each individual to be constantly positioned towards the mourning situations—points of extreme pain and suffering—and address and remove them by managing their knowledge-giving deficiencies.

I have to admit, this is not easy, especially at the start. The force-based system is so much easier. It is so much easier for me to sit in my warm room, watching television, sipping a hot drink, and not spending a moment of my thoughts on other humans in the same city without a warm room and having nothing to eat. Even if the television news gives a quick blurb about them, I dismiss it as the case of people who do not pay attention to their own lives, do not work hard, do not get educated, and fall into the trap of habits like drug abuse and poverty. I see the poor deserving what they get for capabilities they have not developed and shared. With such mindset the mourning situation persists and my thoughts, at best, wander into the idea that the taxes I am paying should help them out. I am already paying the government to take care of the society's "poor." But most prominent on my mind is the comfort of my own situation.

If the news persists a bit longer with the situation of the poor, I switch to another channel, continue to sip my hot drink. Yes, no wonder there is such high interest in rejecting what the divine teaches, not allowing it enter the human way of life. We love "ease" more than anything else and if brute force is the easiest way of creating ease, then that would be the way of life. I am of the opinion that if there were no eschaton and the earth came only in one version, the divine would not have given us the Sermon on the Mount. A divine being would be the first to know of the human addiction to the ease of the force-based life. But the eschaton is on its way and the force-based system is completely unsuited to deal with earth's radical change. The human way of life has to change to the knowledge-based way of the divine teaching if humans are to prosper under the canopied skies.

Which way of life would a wise human choose?

During the past forty years, as I tried to manage my knowledge base, bring into it the divine whispers, many times I faced the inevitable question of the "human wisdom" facing the "divine wisdom." Throughout history and in every earthly society, at any knowledge level, the force-based resource taking system is a product of the human wisdom in managing the application of force and allocation of resources. It is an "ease-focused" wisdom that finds "brute force" the easiest method and best ingredient for managing the human affairs and interactions. The divine wisdom, as given in the Sermon on the Mount, is "knowledge focused" especially on knowledge-giving deficiencies.

The "knowledge giving" links the human to all other humans. It creates many connections that today's force-based system readily ignores. Knowledge giving demands knowledge seeking, knowledge sharing, and knowledge processing. They are all "hard work." We have all experienced that. Whether as student or teacher we all know how hard it is to teach or to learn. So, given the choice between the ease of brute force and the discomfort of knowledge, which path of wisdom are we to choose?

The human history is clear that we prefer the ease-based human wisdom over the discomfort-based divine wisdom. That is what we have done for millennia. In fact, it is the prime sales pitch of those that oppose the Sermon on the Mount. To give the specifics, here is the typical listing of how the traditionalists present the progression of possible meanings of the Sermon on the Mount for human life:[31]

1. The commands of the Sermon on the Mount should be interpreted literally and applied universally and absolutely to everyone and every situation.

2. The commands of the Sermon on the Mount should be modified if they are to be applied to human life.

3. The demands of the Sermon on the Mount should be toned down because the divine used hyperbole in order to dramatize his demands.

4. The intent of the divine in the Sermon on the Mount was on general principles and not specific situations. It is the general principles that are being taught through specific situations. Therefore the specific commands must be translated into general principles and then applied to human life.

5. What the divine is teaching is not about human action but the inner spirit that is beyond the world of human action.

6. The Sermon on the Mount should be read as applicable to two separate groups of humans (the religion business's preferred interpretation). The radical commandments are obligations to be met by the select few. The general instructions are options for the masses. The Sermon on the Mount thus becomes a double-standard view of the divine word.

7. Human life consists of temporal and spiritual domains. In the spiritual domain the human must obey all commands of the Sermon on the Mount. Within the temporal world, however, the human can follow common sense.

8. Instead of seeking meaning in the Sermon on the Mount itself, seek meaning by reference to other material in the New and Old Testament.

9. The Sermon on the Mount is not about either the current life or an ideal future life. They are commands for an interim transitional period brought about by Eschaton. Since the interim period that the divine had expected has long passed with no arrival of Eschaton, then they are no longer applicable to normal human life.

10. The Sermon on the Mount was written for a different age. Some of it might be applicable in current age. All of it would be applicable in a world yet to come.

11. The purpose of the Sermon on the Mount is to bring humans to knowledge of their sinfulness and thus to repentance.

12. The commands of the Sermon on the Mount are absolute and unconditional, but humans must make adjustments because of earthly and human limitations.

I note that the above views of the Sermon on the Mount either make it applicable to only a few humans and thus irrelevant in the daily life of everyone, or assume that humans can modify and change whatever the Sermon on the Mount says. The focus is completely on making the Sermon on the Mount irrelevant to the masses or relevant to the select few. Either way, the Sermon on the Mount is rejected as the human way of life.

All of these views originate at "human wisdom." Two thousand years of human wisdom says throw away the Sermon on the Mount and do not go near it. Can it be right? Is it possible that the human wisdom is better than the divine wisdom? I have to raise this question because for two thousand years humans have chosen to follow the human wisdom when facing the Sermon on the Mount. From all studies I have done I have identified only one glaring problem with human wisdom; resolve that and there would be no need to listen to the Sermon on the Mount. What is that problem? The only problem with the ease of following a force-based way of life is that it <u>concentrates force</u>. Just in case you're not clear about "concentrated force," as an example think armies or nuclear weapons. Can humans manage concentrated force? If humans cannot manage concentrated force, at some point they are all going to face each other with concentrated force in a dance of mutual destruction.

In the eyes of the divine, the human is a choice maker. The way of life is a human choice. If so, why would the divine interfere in something that even the divine knows is the human choice? Is that why the human rejects the Sermon on the Mount? I can argue that there is no divine interference. The divine only clarifies the spectrum of human choice in relation to earth's two versions about which humans, presently, are completely ignorant. At this time, ignorant of the canopied earth, the best humans can do is to throw around words like eschaton and end-of-the-world and that is where the conversation ends. Staying in an ignorance-based position is not good for choice making. That is why the Sermon on the Mount, as choice-based foundational knowledge, informs without interfering.

In the business world's operations, the Sermon on the Mount is so foundational that it is already implementing it everywhere on earth. The only difference that knowing the Sermon on the Mount makes is to make us fully aware of what we do. Yet human awareness of the foundation of life is nothing but a human choice, no different than the items sitting on the supermarket shelf awaiting the human choice. For two thousand years we have chosen to reject such knowledge and might continue to do so even when knowing that the divine wisdom will be of value when facing the eschaton of the earth's transition between its two versions.

The interface between the human and divine wisdoms is inevitable. While we may choose to follow the path set by human wisdom, human wisdom is always encased within the foundation that the divine wisdom provides. Simplistically, the earth is an outcome of the divine wisdom and whatever we do happens within the earth. We have already seen this phenomenon in the business world. For emphasis, let me repeat what I have already said. The business world is where humans spend all their lives. We apply and share much of our capabilities in the workplace the business world sets up and manages. We buy the goods and services we need for daily life at stores the business world sets up and operates. We live in the house built by the business world, eat the food created by the business world, take the medicine prepared by the business world, and breathe the heated or cooled air created by the heating and air conditioning units the business world has built. In short, we are born into the business world— we live in it and die in it. The business world, for thousands of years, has followed the force-based path of ease set by human wisdom. Yet, we know it is impossible to prevent the divine wisdom from entering into the business world even though it has been built, operated, and maintained by force-based human wisdom. In everything the business world does, in bringing humans together as workers, suppliers, and consumers, and in transferring resources to government to keep it functional, the business world is incessantly addressing its knowledge-giving deficiencies. It stays a knowledge seeker and knowledge sharer aligned to a large degree with the first beatitude.

Let me now switch to the second beatitude and test your memory of what I have already said about the business world. To what extent does the business world align itself with the second beatitude? The answer: by quite a bit. In the business world all supply and demand considerations are acts of "mourning management." I know I would be mourning seriously if I did not have food to eat, a bed to sleep in, or pharmaceuticals. The business world is dedicated to ensuring no such mourning possibilities exist. Yet the business world knows nothing of the second beatitude. Would the business world manage its affairs better if it knew the foundational knowledge in the Sermon on the Mount? When goods and services go bad, adversely affecting the human life, leading to mourning situations, would the business world return to knowledge seeking and knowledge sharing more quickly if it knew the problem resides in knowledge-giving deficiencies? This line of questions is all about the "interface." The human, as choice maker, facing the divine as "foundation provider."

The situation is no different than parents providing a home for children. The home is the foundation within which the children interact and conduct life. Any interaction sits at the interface between the foundation and choice-making. I know by personal experience, at times I had to step in and provide more knowledge, telling my child the reasons that climbing up the bookcase would not be a good choice when interacting with the foundation I as parent had provided in the form of a house. From this perspective, the Sermon on the Mount is the flow of knowledge clarifying the human interaction with the divine-provided foundation.

Humans are poor in managing the choice-making interface with the divine-provided foundation. Our choice making and our understanding of the divine-provided foundation come with knowledge-giving deficiencies immersed in ignorance that embeds all things we make and use in life. Nonetheless, we cannot escape the divine-human interface. We cannot escape the connection between the choice-maker and the foundation-provider. Thus the business world, even when unaware of the divine teaching in the Sermon on the Mount, remains a partial practitioner of the divine teaching. It continues to address the knowledge-giving deficiencies and seeks to identify and address the possibilities for mourning situations. The human wisdom remains embedded in the divine wisdom. There is no exception. Yet, how the interface gets set up is the human choice. To use the divine wisdom fully, knowingly, or partially while remaining ignorant of the interface and its significance is a human choice.

A moment of self-reflection

As I write this book, at times I feel I am "telling you" to choose the way of the Sermon on the Mount; that you must choose, that you should choose, and that you have no alternative but the Sermon on the Mount. I am really sorry for that tone. I have no intention of doing so, yet at times it creeps into my writing. I should only tell you about what I know in the societal sharing system, canopied earth, and the Sermon on the Mount. How you use it and what you do with it should be your business and choice. So, anytime you feel I am getting into the must or should mode, please ignore me. If the divine says it is all your choice, I, the speck of dust in the wake of the divine sandals, cannot say otherwise.

V

Understand the Third Step

From knowledge-giving deficiencies and being able to mourn we arrive at the third beatitude:

> 5:5 Blessed are the meek: for they shall inherit the earth.

What is meek? Who is meek? Should we choose to be or not be the meek? With every beatitude, the emphasis is on the human as "choice maker." In the Sermon on the Mount the divine continually highlights a single fact: the divine is not *commanding* the human to do anything. The divine only provides the knowledge of alternatives. We can choose to recognize and address the knowledge-giving deficiencies, or not. We can identify and address situations of intense pain and suffering, or not. Whether it is knowledge-giving deficiency or the mourning situation, it is addressed where and when humans face the application of force and allocation of resource in relation to alternatives. Assessing alternatives and making choices among alternatives is the essence of choice-making. Every human should be good at that. The third beatitude teaches the conduct of "choice making."

Thing making

Acts of force and resource management depend on the level of societal knowledge and individual knowledge processing capabilities. This creates a variety of earthly societies, some skilled in managing force such that no brute force is used in human interactions in contrast to others that heavily rely on the use of brute force. Managing force and assessing alternatives demands knowledge management. What else can I tell you about knowledge management? How can we develop a deeper, knowledge-based understanding of human existence? How can we understand the human as knowledge seeker and knowledge processor?

To answer the questions we need to start with the human as "thing maker." All things humans make and use are composites of knowledge and earth material. They take shape within the matrix of interactions defined by the force-based resource taking system. Everything humans make and use is a "knowledge-packet." Whether a sandwich, house, computer, toilet paper, airplane, university, or nation, they are all "things" or "knowledge-packets," composites of knowledge and earth material. We have to learn to see life as a "world of things," a "world of knowledge-packets," made and used by humans. It is hard to do so because we have not done it previously. At present we are not comfortable with the knowledge-based way of life.

Humans live within the "world of things." They live within the "world of knowledge-packets" they collectively bring into existence. What is unique about things humans make and use? We all do it; we all know it. In all things humans make and use, the human never knows everything about that "thing." Every "thing" the human makes and uses has "ignorance" as a component. I know how to drive a car, but have no knowledge of how to make it. The maker of the car knows how to make it but has no way of knowing how to prevent it from falling apart year after year. Ignorance eats away at everything humans make and use.

This leads to a foundational observation. Everything humans make and use originates at two components: what the <u>human knows</u> and what the <u>human does not know</u>. What the human knows I name "knowledge" and what the human does not know "ignorance." Can we see that everything humans make and use is a composite of knowledge and ignorance? There is no exception to this mixture in human life. The human is as much the manager of knowledge as the manager of ignorance. This makes the human the converter of ignorance to knowledge. The human sits at the interface of two domains, one ignorance the other knowledge. Life happens at that interface. All knowledge-giving deficiencies in human life have their origin in the "ignorance content" of knowledge-packets. We see that every day in the goods and services humans make and use.

When talking about the human as converter of ignorance to knowledge, as maker and manager of composites of ignorance and knowledge, the prominent "thing," the starting point is always the "word." Every "word" humans create and use is a "thing," a composite of knowledge and ignorance. The word is the most elemental knowledge-packet humans create in their lives. The "word," thought, spoken or written, is the thing—the knowledge-packet—most frequently made and used by humans.

The best way to understand knowledge management in human life is to become familiar with high-ignorance-content words that humans make and use regularly. I refer to these words as "suitcase words." By themselves, they have little meaning—offer little knowledge—because they are empty shells in the manner of an empty suitcase. Some meaning comes from the shell of the suitcase, but the meaning of the suitcase word comes primarily from what one puts into the suitcase. This implies that the word can acquire all sorts of meaning depending on the suitcase content. The human awareness of suitcase words is critical to knowledge processing and ignorance management, essential to well-being of the societal sharing system.

Meeting the "suitcase words" when managing knowledge

The "suitcase word" is a word. By itself it has little meaning—little knowledge content. It achieves meaning from the knowledge added by the individual using it.[32] You'll find it intriguing that examples of suitcase words include democracy, freedom, justice, peace and similar words. The point is not whether these words are good or bad. Humans often lean strongly toward seeing them as good. The point is that the suitcase words are low-knowledge-content things. They say very little by themselves and can be interpreted and assigned meaning in a variety of different ways.

The suitcase words when used as high-ignorance-content things will dilute the knowledge content in human interactions and can adversely affect human life. But the use of the suitcase words is not always bad. In the short-term, they can also grease the wheels life. If we are promised democracy and freedom, we become more optimistic about life seeing it flow more smoothly toward the desired destination. This makes human understanding and use of suitcase words critical to human well-being. This is why the human must manage ignorance. The human is both knowledge manger and ignorance manager. The mixing of knowledge and ignorance gives rise to infinite alternatives in human life. The choice maker faces the infinite ways of mixing knowledge and ignorance.

Suitcase words can be used individually or combined with other words to produce "stacked suitcase words." The greater the stacking, the more meaningless the arrangement becomes as the stacking amplifies the ignorance content. We should be most interested in awareness and management of stacked suitcase words because many important words used in daily life are suitcase words. They do not carry a single meaning recognized by everyone. They possess meanings assigned according to each individual's views, biases, and preferences. The individual decides which pieces of knowledge are relevant and are to be placed in the suitcases.

The ignorance content of the suitcase creates "commonality."

Everyone loves "freedom." Everyone relates to "democracy." This makes the suitcase words the pacifiers humans need in life. Ignorance is a pacifier in human life even though life is built on the hard work of converting ignorance into knowledge. The ignorance traps the human while the knowledge frees. The two have to be managed together.

Here is another twist. Knowledge is not the only thing the human adds to the suitcase. One can also add ignorance or misinformation. Misinformation is a bad form of knowledge. One can even make the suitcase larger without putting anything in it, thus increasing its empty space as ignorance content. Making the suitcase larger undermines its meager knowledge content, making it more meaningless. This is often done through addition of "weasel words,"[33,34,35] though the stacking of the suitcase words achieves the same result.

What are weasel words? Examples are words like: possibly, probably, arguably, people say …, there is evidence that …, and it is known that …. Thus if I say, "Freedom is essential to human life," it is already a stack of the suitcase words freedom, essential, and life. What do we mean by freedom, or essential, or life? The statement does not carry much knowledge. But I can lower whatever knowledge is present by adding weasel words. I can say, "Probably freedom is essential to human life," or "It is known that freedom is essential to human life." Or, I can make it even more meaningless by saying, "It is arguably known that freedom is probably essential to human life." Each step creating a knowledge-packet with higher ignorance content.

By now, in human interactions, the pernicious side of the weasel and suitcase words should be evident. Such awareness is essential to creating high-knowledge-content things when sharing force, resources, knowledge, and direction setting. It is important to minimize the unintended or dysfunctional flow of ignorance into whatever we collectively do in the societal sharing system that sustains us all. Life is always built on high-knowledge-content things, thus human must have a reason to choose a high-ignorance-content way of life.

The never-ending reality: the knowledge processing, the conversion of ignorance to knowledge, and ignorance management never end. Every word comes with its "ignorance content," some more, some less. We can better understand the ignorance content if we see the word as a human-made thing no different than the water bottle or the automobile. In the same manner that the water bottle and automobile come into existence from shared capabilities, so does the "word."

Every word comes into existence within the context of the societal sharing system. The challenge is we have a harder time seeing the connection of "word" to the shared capabilities of millions of others because everyone accepts the illusion that the individual alone is the creator of the word just spoken, written down, or read. Yet every word is just another "thing" made and used within the societal sharing system. It can only exist if sustained by the shared capabilities of millions. The ease with which humans create and use words gives rise to the illusion that it does not involve others.

Consider another view of "word." All goods and services humans make and use in daily life are composites of words and earth material. Everything is a composite of words and earth material. Take the words away from anything, be it a computer, car, sandwich, or toilet paper, and all that would be left is a pile of earth material. Humans combine words with earth material to create things like bridges, houses, pens, books, and airplanes. When any of the goods and services fail, especially over time, they do so because of the ignorance content of the words used in creating them.

To exist, especially to exist well, it is important to recognize that every aspect of human life is a mix of things humans know (knowledge) and things humans do not know (ignorance). There is no exception to this fact of human life. The mixture of knowledge and ignorance creates every alternative in human life. To be able to manage any aspect of human life one must be equally good at managing the ignorance and knowledge contents of goods and services that define the daily human needs in life. All goods and services are "knowledge-packets," each with its own ignorance content. From this perspective, the workplace, government, and even the societal sharing system is a knowledge-packet, each with its own ignorance content, created and maintained by humans as ignorance to knowledge converters and choice makers.

We are not accustomed to looking at an old, broken down car and saying, "the ignorance content did it," but we should be. We are not focused on the reduction of ignorance content; not focused on having a car that lasts for decades, designed to readily incorporate new pieces of knowledge. Instead we are complacent with the "ignorance content" we already have in our knowledge-packets, the ignorance content that continually breaks everything down. We continue replacing many knowledge-packets every few years and in doing so waste resources and human capabilities through repetition.

Repetition is often ignorance-driven repetition. My favorite demonstration of ignorance-driven repetition is the picture of the lone house standing on the beach in the aftermath of a hurricane. All other houses have been swept away, leaving their construction to be repeated. The lone house is the only one that paid attention to its ignorance content in relation to hurricanes. It was designed so that it would withstand a hurricane, a house with higher knowledge content compared to others. It lasted longer in the face of adversity, a graphic and key lesson of the role ignorance content plays in human life—a lesson no one should forget.

How to decide good and bad?

In assessing alternatives when managing force or resources, humans continually make *good-not good* decisions. Which alternative is good, which alternative is not good. Humans are force appliers and resource takers. They are also *good-not good decision makers*. We need to understand how humans, individually and societally, make good-not good decisions.

Humans exercise good-not good decision making in creation

and use of every knowledge-packet. Be it a loaf of bread, a computer, a community, a complex society, or the simple and mundane things like when should one get up and what is good to eat for lunch, there is not a single aspect of human life that does not involve good-not good decision making. It is always a matter of the choice maker selecting among alternatives. By understanding the individual and society from the good-not good decision making perspective, humans improve the ability to analyze the force-based resource taking system, the ability to understand the exchange-based resource taking system, and the ability to understand life, especially from the point of view of the Sermon on the Mount.

The individual and societal good-not good distinctions take place in different domains. The society may have no interest in making good-not good decisions as to what I eat for breakfast. The way I eat breakfast is my "few-agree position." But the society does make good-not good decisions as to the speed at which I drive my car. The speed is a "many-agree position" that the society enforces as if an "all-agree position." All of the "few-agree" and "many-agree" positions are outcomes of good-not good decisions. They are all alternatives that appear in human life and must be managed. That I like to eat chocolate every day is my few-agree position. It originates in my good-not good decision making. That on the highway I drive around 70 miles per hour is my alignment with a societal many-agree position. It originates at societal good-not good decision making. The formation of few-agree and many-agree positions is a key aspect of good-not good decision making at both the individual and societal levels. What does this mean for managing force and resources?

Humans have had millennia of practice in observing and determining the best application of good-not good decision making in force management. As a result, a societal structure has emerged based on backing certain important many-agree positions with the societal concentrated force, turning them into "all-agree" societal positions. We give the societal all-agree positions names like laws and rules and in modern times often justify such force management as democratic rule of the majority.

The unexpected outcome is that the laws become the society's highest level of good-not good decision making. I repeat for emphasis, the laws are the highest level of good-not good decision making in the society. The laws reflect the highest level of good-not good decision making in the societal sharing system. They are the most important good-not good decisions of the society. I bet you did not know that, a truly unexpected outcome. The concentrated force is primarily directed at protecting such many-agree positions. The brute force that declares them all-agree, makes everyone in the society adhere to them.

Not every all-agree position is structurally "all-agree." Often no more than 51% of the society has agreed to the all-agree position, but the other 49% is forced to abide by the many-agree position of 51%. It is most important to understand that in the current force-based method of managing the many-agree positions, the all-agree positions are "force-backed many-agree positions." They are created and maintained by "brute force."

In order to manage the society's mix of many-agree positions, all societies set up organizational structures we know by names like the House of Representatives and Senate. Currently, all such arrangements are focused on using brute force to push one group's many-agree position against others instead of managing the collective of alternatives that face the society as many-agree positions. Rather than adopting a patient and gentle way of knowledge processing in order to combine and modify the many-agree positions to serve the needs of the masses for goods and services, the purpose is to apply brute force to make everyone abide by the many-agree position that has just reached the 51% position. This method relies on brute force in the guise of managing the society's many-agree positions.

In many societies there is no need to worry about the 51% method of managing the many-agree positions as everyone responds to the "power-backed few-agree positions" that set the all-agree positions for everyone. There, the use of brute force in managing the many-agree positions is most evident in the powerful dictatorial individual or group that rules and manages the society's many-agree positions. So long as human societies have not learned their key societal challenge as "management of many-agree positions," the game of reaching the 51% and then applying brute force on 49% to follow the way of the 51% is the best humans can do. It is a knowledge-deficient and eventually destructive way of managing many-agree positions where the societies will continue to degrade and self-destroy in the battlefield of many-agree positions managed through brute force.

Despite its glaring deficiencies in management of society's many-agree positions, in all societies the pragmatic purpose of law is twofold. First, to protect wealth, and second, to protect the few-agree positions of individuals. The societal wealth and the society's "sea of few-agree positions" are bounded and protected by laws. This should not be taken as laws having permanence or approaching perfection. By now we know laws are human-made things with their own ignorance content. Often they will have to change and adjust as the society changes its knowledge base.

Let me summarize the good-not good decision making. In human societies the simple picture of good-not good decision making divides into two categories, two alternatives: many-agree and few-agree. Some many-agree positions are backed by the societal concentrated force. They become the all-agree positions we know as rules, laws, and regulations. I prefer to call the all-agree positions "force extensions." A word like "law" does not tell us that we are dealing with force management. The word "force extension" does. All societies are deficient in managing their many-agree positions. The managers of the society's many-agree positions, those elected or appointed to the society's House of Representatives and the Senate, are more dedicated to fighting and forcing one another than working collectively to manage the society's mix of many-agree positions. This is a serious knowledge-giving deficiency at the highest societal level.

The management of the many-agree positions also includes the management of the few-agree positions. The individual few-agree positions cannot be given the backing of the societal concentrated force to turn them into force extensions. Why? Because only few humans would agree to abide by those positions. The few-agree positions exist within the domain of individuals and small groups. Though not backed by the societal force to become force extensions, the few-agree positions are *protected* by the societal force through force extensions. That is not a universal condition. At times an individual, some individuals, or a small group seeks ways of turning their few-agree positions into all-agree positions. Occasionally they succeed. The prominent example is the dictator and the ruling elite. Their "power-backed few-agree positions" become the law of the land. The prime ingredient in power-backed few-agree positions is "brute force."

Where does "ethics and morality" fit in all this? If everything in human life is good-not good decision making, then ethics and morality are forms of good-not good decision making. The "ethics" and "morality" are a word-based labeling game played by humans in relation to many-agree positions. Some many-agree positions, and at times some few-agree positions, carry the ethics and morality labels. The many-agree positions labeled as "ethics and morality" are in the first tier of many-agree positions vying to be considered as "law." In this process a good number of many-agree and few-agree positions strive to rise to the level of being recognized as ethics and morality. This means the few-agree, many-agree, and all-agree positions are symbiotically linked. All many-agree positions originate from a base of few-agree positions. All few-agree and many-agree positions are symbiotically linked to laws, the force extensions. The force extensions (laws) are the society's highest level of good-not good decision making.

Looking through the lens of ethics and morality, what is significant? That we must see and understand the force extensions—the rules, laws, and regulations—as the society's highest "moral and ethical positions." The society considers them to possess such high level of significance that it must back them by its concentrated force in order to give them the "all-agree status." The laws are the society's highest levels of ethics and morality. Surprised? Nonetheless, this is not universal. It does not mean that the few-agree positions cannot be backed by the societal force and declared the society's laws. In fact, that is what the dictators do. In all this, the "brute force" is the prime player, the key ingredient. There is no gentleness in brute force, thus no meekness in the laws. The meek would avoid the laws as none are gentle. Is that ever possible in human life, living without laws?

Who else pushes laws? Among the culprits are the society's managers, those that manage the business world. They are inclined to find ways of putting their own few-agree positions into law. Such behavior is not new. It is ancient. Adam Smith noted this behavior about two hundred years ago. He was adamant as to how the society should consider any law proposal that originates at the business world's managers.

> As their thoughts, however, are commonly exercised rather about the interest of their own particular branch of business, than about that of the society.
>
> ...
>
> The proposal of any new law or regulation of commerce which comes from this order, ought always to be listened to with great precaution, and ought never to be adopted till after having been long and carefully examined, not only with the most scrupulous, but with the most suspicious attention.[36]

Hmm, has anyone listened? I don't think so. From business lobbyists in the legislative system we know that the current design of the societal sharing system is not capable of heeding Adam Smith's advice. The power-backed few-agree positions continue to become the laws and pretend to be among the society's highest levels of ethics and morality. It's a shame. It is the worst way of bringing brute force into the human life, the worst way of not being meek. It undermines the societal sharing system, yet it is a feature of the human as "good-not good decision maker."

In summary, the outcome of the good-not good decision

making is first the few-agree and many-agree positions. Then some many-agree positions are converted into force extensions. We already know that in the current design of the societal sharing system this would be the ideal, expected path but not the actual outcome. The actual outcome has a sprinkling of power-backed few-agree positions.

What else do we know about good-not good decision making? Let us focus on the process of converting many-agree positions into force-backed all-agree positions. To become an all-agree position, a many-agree position has to satisfy "resource balance" requirements. An all-agree position binds the society to specific levels of resource expenditures. At minimum it sets the required concentrated force to maintain the force extensions. The *resource implications* of converting a many-agree position into a force-backed all-agree position have to be fully considered. Does the society have the resources? Where do the resources come from?

When only a few individuals agree on a good-not good position, the situation is in the individualized domain of good-not good positions. No societal consideration of resource implications needs to be made. The situation lies in the sea of few-agree positions. The individuals can do as they wish with their resources. For example, at present, the good-not good position that demands the human societies abandon the nuclear weapons is a few-agree position. The all-agree position sees the concentrated force and nuclear weapons as needed and good. The society has assessed and provided the resources needed to create and maintain such weapons. It has decided that such resources are available and can be spent on production and maintenance of nuclear weapons. Consider the comparative point of view: many societal resources flow into the many-agree position that creates and maintains the nuclear weapons but little if any societal resources flow into the few-agree position of not having the nuclear weapons.

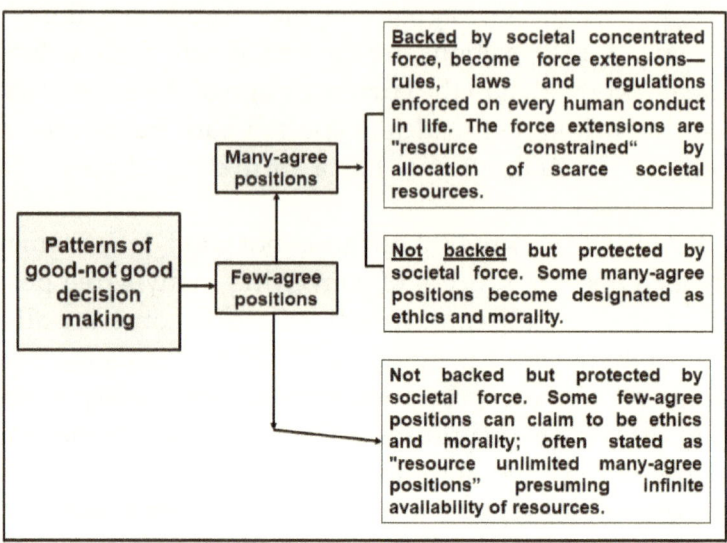

Consider another situation, a paradox at first glance, but not so. Consider the good-not good position that "all humans are created equal." It has the *appearance* of a "many agree" if not an all-agree position when in fact it is a "few agree" position. The "many agree" illusion comes from two directions. First, words like equal and human are suitcase words, and second, the position's resource requirements have not been considered. The word "equal" comes with a huge suitcase. Even the word "human" has a big suitcase. With resource consideration we would immediately see the initial many-agree position transform into few-agree positions. For example, when we say all humans are equal, do we mean they all receive the same salary? Each will have a house? Each will drive a new car? If we say no to such questions, then the notion of equality drops from all-agree to many-agree and from there to few-agree positions. However, if we answer yes, then we have to identify from where the society obtains the resources to achieve such equality.

Resource consideration is an act of knowledge processing in relation to the suitcase words embedded in good-not good decisions. The resource-based knowledge processing changes the seemingly many-agree yet high-ignorance-content statement of "universal equality" into a few-agree statement. This is a foundational view of the human as good-not good decision maker. In every society, in all times, under all conditions and circumstances, good-not good decision making leads to few-agree, many-agree, and all-agree force-backed positions that the society has to maintain and manage. Few-agree, many-agree, and all-agree positions constitute a simple model of good-not good decision making. They are "alternatives" available to humans. The divine suggests that we take time and avoid brute force when developing and choosing among those alternatives.

We know the force extensions are the rules, laws, and regulations that all humans are to obey regardless of how they organize themselves. They are "brute force" mandates. Whether at the workplace or with family, the force extensions are force-backed moral obligations for everyone. Their good-not good question has already been decided societally. The society feels so strongly about such moral positions that they are backed by the society's concentrated force.

That is the theory, the practice of which depends on human capabilities, especially the capability to create and maintain force extensions. This is no different than any other thing humans make and use. All "things" face the same situation. For example, those that do not have the capability to make, operate, and maintain automobiles, cannot and do not do so. Regardless of how much theoretical knowledge is available to them, they are not capable of making automobiles. The same is true for many-agree positions and force extensions. Like making automobiles, it is the application of capabilities that turns the few-agree positions into moral positions and then into force extensions. In the same manner that making the automobile is a question of resource balance, so is the making of force extensions. The automaker would go bankrupt and stop making cars if it cannot balance the flow of resources in its operations. The same is true of force extensions. An assessment of resource requirements is intrinsic to turning the many-agree position into a force extension. Every force extension is a demand

for societal behavior and as such every force extension has
resource implications. The force extensions that cannot maintain
the societal resource balance are ignored and discarded. They fall
apart no different than an abandoned factory that cannot make
automobiles.

Every many-agree position must consider the well-being of
the society's resource taking processes before being adopted as
force extension. There is no such societal requirement for few-
agree positions or even the many-agree positions that will not be
considered as force extensions. The resource questions on few-
agree good-not good decisions are limited to the individuals that
adopts it. If an individual strongly feels that the human should live
a certain lifestyle, it is that person's resources that support action
along that good-not good position. There is no consideration of
spending the society's resources to make everyone do the same. If
that individual fails to provide the needed resources, that lifestyle
gets abandoned, becoming only a tiny blip in the sea of few-agree
positions.

Yet that is not a complete picture. The sea of few-agree
positions, to exist, has to be limited and protected by "brute force."
Then the design is not gentle even though the purpose is to protect
the individual's uniqueness in life. The sea of few-agree positions
is the collection of societally-allowed few-agree positions. The
mechanism for allowing or disallowing a few-agree position is
determined by brute force. Brute force does not allow the few-
agree position of using cocaine, but allows the few-agree position
of eating French pastries. It may seem the desired and effective
way of managing the societal few-agree positions, yet it is not
gentle as it relies heavily on concentrated brute force. The design
of the sea of few-agree positions is not meek, not gentle. It reeks
with brute force. Can humans ever do otherwise? At this time,
mired in the force-based way of life, it seems almost impossible to
manage force in ways that no brute force would ever be applied
on humans.

Manager-managed duality as direction setting

If brute force is so prevalent in human life, an ingredient in every alternative that humans develop and adopt, and if the societal sharing system is built on the shared capabilities of everyone, then how do millions of humans set direction for one another or come to adopt shared directions? History makes the answer clear. In every society the force network acts as the "command structure." A few at the top control and manage the society's force network. Everyone else becomes a follower.

What about the production and exchange of goods and services within the societal force network? It is also built upon sharing the individual capabilities to provide what humans need in daily life. In every society, the individual has some degree of freedom as to where and how to share one's capabilities in the societal sharing system. However, there is no guarantee that such freedom will be large, and often it is small and confined by brute force and resource requirements. In all this the incessant fact is that "sharing" requires "organizing" and humans differ in their capability to organize. Some are really good, most stink. The act of organizing requires resources. Those that excel in obtaining and managing resources use them in production of goods and services and are rewarded for doing so. They are the ones that pile up the personal resources we know as wealth.

Wealth is a key artifact in human life at both individual and societal levels. Wealth always functions as means of organizing and amplifying the human capabilities. It also divides the society into managers and managed, the direction-setters and direction-followers. It creates the manager-managed duality. This is the same arrangement as the one used in setting up and controlling the societal force network. Those that have or control wealth become "managers." Everyone else becomes the "managed." The manager-managed duality creates the capability sharing arrangement that produces goods and services for the daily needs of all.

As command structure, manager-managed duality manifests in every aspect of the society, especially in the societal sharing system where the force extensions support and protect voluntary exchange-based resource taking. In theory this is wonderful. It turns the societal sharing system into an organic, self-sustaining being that takes care of everyone's daily needs. In practice, the degree of success in setting up and using this system depends on the size of the societal knowledge base. Moreover, it depends on the knowledge processing capabilities of individuals. More importantly, it depends on the societal ability to manage brute force. As such, every societal sharing system comes with its own measure of meekness. The more a society uses brute force, the less gentle it is, and the more distant it becomes from being meek.

The force extensions come with illusion of meekness. So long as everyone's behavior remains aligned with force extensions, it is as if there is no brute force. Sounds simple and practical, yet there are many societies that cannot create and maintain an extended force network. They frequently revert to using brute force as the only means of managing the society's daily affairs. So easy to imagine a society relying on brute force for managing the daily affairs as everyone carries a weapon and everyone worries about others carrying weapons. Everyone organizes to kill and be killed. In the extreme no one organizes to produce goods and services for anyone.

This makes the force-immersed society quite inefficient in organizing to provide for the needs of all. Many go hungry and without the basics of life. Worse, they are constantly exposed to the brute force of those that want to improve their own resource position through controlling the meager resources and capabilities of others. Nonetheless, even in the most decrepit society, the manager-managed duality remains the only way that a large number of humans can manage their daily lives. The top manager might be a dictator that only knows how to kill humans in order to keep their behavior in line. That only reflects the society's degree of capability in development and use of force extensions. It reflects the mode of utilization of manager-managed duality, the size of the societal knowledge base, and the extent of individual capabilities for production and distribution of goods and services.

Regardless of how good or how bad it might get, every society exists within the force-based resource taking system. There is no possibility for getting rid of the manager-managed duality, even when the manager is a deranged, murderous dictator. The challenge for that society is not to find something to replace the manager-managed duality. The challenge is to increase the knowledge-base size and the knowledge processing capabilities of individuals so that an extended force network can be set up to support and protect the societally shared capabilities directed at voluntary, exchange-based resource taking. Many societies have grave difficulties in achieving that. This means many societies are quite distant from the meek behavior.

I am always surprised that it is so easy to measure a society's ability to make and use force extensions. The force management capability can be simplistically measured by the society's ability to make things like roads and automobiles. The society incapable of creating good roads and incapable of manufacturing automobiles, in general, is a society incapable of creating and maintaining a functional extended force network. It is not a society that manages brute force well.

All societies reflect the "thing-making capabilities" of humans in the societal sharing system. Whether road, automobile, or force extension, they are all "things." The human is a thing maker with varying skills. But regardless of skill, the society has to organize itself according to the managed-managed duality and the force-based resource taking system. All societies use the same foundational structure, the only difference is some use it well while others use it poorly.

So, where are we? We have arrived at the end point of the operational view of human societies. We have considered force and resource management at a given level of the societal knowledge base. We have seen the management of force and resources within the framework of the individual and societal good-not good decision making. We have a foundational view of the factors that determine human life. Armed with this information we can better approach the divine knowledge in the Sermon on the Mount.

Ahh, we the meek, is that possible?

We can now dig into the third step, the third beatitude, the identification and management of alternatives.

The human is the choice maker. That we know. The divine gives us a glimpse of the human as meek. Choice making and meekness, how are they related?" In the traditional view, meek is an attribute of the poor. We reject that view. We know that the third step relates to knowledge processing, a continuation of the first two steps. From a knowledge processing point of view the main characteristics of "meek" are being *patient* and *gentle*. The patient recognizes the role of "time" in human activities and does not rush. It seeks knowledge of alternatives before acting. The gentle does not apply brute force on others in whatever alternative being considered. The gentle avoid the use of brute force in any alternative, especially the many-agree and few-agree positions that define the individual and societal lives. In a simple, idealistic view, the meek becomes the nonviolent alternative-assessor.

In the third step we encounter "time" and "assessment of alternatives." They are the means of improving knowledge giving and preventing mourning situations. We humans understand the role of "time" in our lives. Time is the human individual's most valuable resource. How it is used and applied greatly matters. Not spending "time" to assess a situation and not being able to compare alternatives form the recipe for living a deficient life. Time allows the development of alternatives, especially gentle alternatives devoid of brute force in human interactions. It allows the possibility for knowledge seeking and knowledge sharing without reliance on brute force as enforcer of human behavior. By rushing, humans would become deficient in knowledge seeking and knowledge sharing. If one rushes, instead of preventing a mourning situation one may only provide a bandage, leaving it to exist, grow, and repeat. To rush with deficient knowledge, the human, almost always, has to force others to share their capabilities. In that case, the sharing cannot be gentle. It would be the brute force dictating the terms of human action and the choice among alternatives. It seems the only time that one may choose not to act as meek is when facing a mourning situation. Facing the mourning situation, the alternatives shrink to one, the mourning situation itself that must be addressed and removed. Can "addressing and removing" present themselves as alternatives? Can that be done gently? I don't know. If a city is being bombed, stopping the bombing is the only alternative and the only gentle thing to do. What about the "hungry" in the city? In answering such questions I face all the dilemmas that a human faces when for thousands of years the society has not given a moment's thought to the beatitudes and everyone's life is but one long road of force-based ways of behavior. That can be so confusing.

In any moment of confusion, we encounter the reminder that human wisdom resides within the foundation of the divine wisdom. I am always intrigued that even when the human is not aware of the Sermon on the Mount, or is aware but chooses not to follow it, still the human life remains partially aligned with the operational beatitudes. Just look at the business world. Everything the business world does happens within the society's extended force network which is backed by concentrated brute force, yet within that setting, to a large degree the business world fits the meek behavior. It takes time to assess its alternatives for application of resources to the production and distribution of goods and services, in general shuns the possibilities of violence within its own borders and in a majority of its products and services, and it pays immediate attention to mourning situations to address and remove them. The meek behavior is everywhere, only it is not consciously pushed to its upper limit. Moreover, the consciousness does not reach into force extensions where the business world heavily relies on brute force.

The human society is a "society of resource takers." Every emergency, every arrangement of singular alternatives is a temptation for excessive resource taking and many humans migrate toward exploiting it. Outside of the family setting, humans often see huge resource taking opportunities when someone or an organization is stuck in an emergency situation and does not have the option of taking time or comparing alternatives. Put in words relevant to the beatitudes, in today's force-based structure, every mourning situation is viewed as a resource taking opportunity, not a situation where pain and suffering are to be immediately removed with all available knowledge and resources. Outside of the family setting this happens at every level of pain and suffering, not limited to bad cases of pain and suffering—the mourning situations.

In minor cases of pain and suffering, like an individual that has locked himself out of the apartment, the time becomes compressed. In the force-based resource taking system those interested in excessive resource taking organize their activities and goods and services around exploiting such conditions at the highest possible level. When a society begins addressing knowledge-giving deficiencies and mourning situations, there would be reduced possibilities for creating excessive resource taking opportunities that tempt certain humans to develop their capabilities along the lines of exploiting others. But still, such exploitation is human choice. The Sermon on the Mount is clear, humans would be happier if they did not exploit such opportunities, but it is a choice. There is no "do not" command in the Sermon on the Mount. It fully recognizes the human condition as choice maker, for good or for bad.

The traditional view has no notion of patience as time management. It does not point at gentleness in assessment and selection among alternatives. Instead, meekness is a desired ethical concept practiced by few. The traditional view sees meek as a suitcase word equated with another suitcase word "humility." This only highlights one thing, the traditional view immersed in ignorance unable to see the gentle, patient assessment of alternatives by humans as choice makers. In the traditional view the only alternative for knowledge processing is to jump from one suitcase word to another. In this process it has to rely on words with large empty suitcases like humility, the sign of facing ignorance and not knowing what to do; the sign of no desire or intention for working hard at conversion of ignorance to knowledge so that the suitcases can be filled.

In the third beatitude, the meek behavior, the gentle, patient assessment and selection of alternatives, is promised a vivid outcome. It will lead to inheriting the earth. What does that mean? The word "earth" is left an empty suitcase. It could be the earth as it is today, the blue-skied earth, or it could be the canopied earth, or it could be a reference to both. The way the Sermon on the Mount is offered to humans, it is logical to assume that it includes both earth versions. More interesting is the word "inherit." How are we to understand this part of the divine teaching? Within the human context the word "inherit" always refers to an individual, group, or generation receiving resources and acquiring features from the previous individual, group, or generation.

Consider today's reality, the reality of shared capabilities that create today's societal sharing system. What is the first item of inheritance that shines above all others? Is it wealth? Is it knowledge? Or, is it today's force-based system that comes with a "destruction switch." It comes with the possibility of leaving nothing to future humans. Zero inheritance. In its simplest form imagine the destruction switch as the stockpile of the nuclear weapons. How does that kind of inheritance compare with what we are told in the Sermon on the Mount? The third beatitude tells us that there is "no destruction switch" in the "meek" as it shuns brute force in all alternatives it chooses in life. That way, the patient and gentle treatment of alternatives always leaves the earth for the future generations. What does this mean? The size of the nuclear stockpiles remains a physical measure of the human dedication to the force-based, non-meek way of life. The bigger it gets, the farther humans get from the way the divine suggests in the Sermon on the Mount. The more humans behave in the manner of meek, the smaller the destruction switch will become, with the possibility that it might disappear. The possibility that the earth will be continually inherited by humans greatly increases.

Let's change our orientation a bit and consider another question.[37] Why wasn't "gentle, patient assessment of alternatives" placed after the first beatitude? It seems logical to address knowledge-giving deficiencies then pay attention to gentle and patient assessment of alternatives. Only after having done that, would humans focus on alternatives for addressing cases of really bad pain and suffering—the mourning situations.[38] Yet, that is not what the divine teaches. True, adopting the attitude of addressing knowledge deficiencies comes first, but immediately next to it is addressing the situations of intense pain and suffering. The intense pain and suffering cannot wait, it cannot endure in time. Time acts as "destroyer" in any situation of intense pain and suffering. With whatever knowledge we have, with whatever knowledge deficiencies we face, we must address the situations of intense pain and suffering and remove them. When the world is devoid of intense pain and suffering, only then can humans patiently and gently assess the alternatives for action. Only then, time becomes a friend and ally.

VI

Deeper Understanding
at the Fourth Step

We have arrived at the fourth step, the fourth beatitude:

> 5:6 Blessed are they which do hunger and thirst after
> righteousness: for they shall be filled.

In the first three steps the focus is on knowledge processing, addressing the mourning situations, and gentle and patient assessment and selection among alternatives. In all these the knowledge-giving deficiencies and alternative selection take place within a specific context, the application of force and allocation of resources. Yet, in the first two steps there is no mention of force application or resource allocation. The application of force, its gentle management, and its focus on discarding brute force makes its first appearance in the third beatitude. But we know that the composite of force and resources are inherent to every aspect of human life. That the Sermon on the Mount starts at awareness of knowledge-giving deficiencies does not nullify the need to manage the application of brute force and allocation of resources. In the final count, even the way of the Sermon on the Mount is a force-based resource taking system. The only difference, it starts with "knowledge-giving deficiencies," not "application of brute force."

Does the fourth step address the force-based resource taking system, and if so, how? In the fourth beatitude we arrive at the word "righteousness," equivalent to "justice." It means "fair management" of application of force and allocation of resources in the life of the human individual and in human societies. It is intriguing that we are left with empty suitcases. How do we fill the suitcases of righteousness, justice, or fairness? We are not told how to achieve justice or achieve fairness. If we start with the first three steps, would it be easier to understand the situation? Let us do that. Let me also stay only with the word "justice" as whatever we see in justice will equally apply to fairness and righteousness.

Justice depends on the knowledge base available to a society. It depends on the knowledge processing capabilities of the society's individuals. Is that why the fourth step, the fourth beatitude, leaves justice totally to human abilities as "force appliers, "resource takers," "choice makers," and "knowledge processors?" When it comes to justice, this is the path that humans have always taken in history. They have always been the decision makers as to what justice is and how it is determined. At every step in human history our knowledge base and knowledge processing capabilities have changed. When all we could do was to swing a sword, justice was different. The sword decided justice. When we created and used force extensions, justice was different. The pen decided justice. The sword sat in the background, rarely called upon to intervene. Based on our knowledge base and knowledge processing capabilities, in every time period and at every situation, we humans have made choices as to the *just direction* that our lives would take.

In the fourth step, the fourth beatitude, the divine knowledge points at the reality that knowledge processing and choice making are intertwined in creation of the human's societal life. The human connections to one another strengthen and multiply the possibilities for being more just, though it is never guaranteed. The message of the fourth step: create your way of just life, your way of force and resource balance. The human is placed in charge. The only radical change the fourth beatitude suggests is for the human to remain utterly and continuously focused on justice. That is different from the force-based system where humans focus on justice is only when an injustice happens. If no injustice, justice sits in the background and does nothing. Why does the divine want us to continuously thirst and hunger after justice? Why not do it when an injustice happens and otherwise leave it alone?

The context, as it exists now

Through the societal sharing system humans make and use everything in their lives. The societal sharing system, the deepest operational foundation of human existence, is valuable, but we need more details. The societal sharing system is built out of four universal dimensions. The first, "force sharing." In its most basic form humans use force to bend and shape the earth material into what humans need in daily life. All goods and services require application of force on earth material. In the manner of the universe, humans are "force appliers." Here is the catch. If as force applier the human directs force only at making goods and services, the force sharing would be easy and straightforward, but that is not the case. Humans also apply force on one another.

When the force is applied to earth material, it digs the ore out of the earth, extracts the metal out of the ore, and shapes the metal into all sorts of things. The earth has little problem with taking on such force, bending to its command. It has done so for billions of years and has faced many force appliers. Such is not the case with humans. Applying brute force on humans does not achieve bending and reshaping but inflicts harm and eventually destroys the human. When applied on humans, brute force and harm go together. The brute force exposure and associated harm have to be avoided if the societal sharing system is to thrive. In the design of the societal sharing system, and more specifically in arranging the force sharing schemes, humans have come up with the ingenious force management technique that serves and not harms the human. I will talk about that later in more detail.

Next is the "resource" dimension. Everything in life is made of the earth material shaped and delivered in forms humans can use. All these are "resources." More important, they are resources that the others provide to an individual for use in life. They are composites of earth material and human capabilities. Every composite of earth material and human capabilities happens as "resource sharing." What belonged to the earth and others is given to me, the individual. Humans share what they create. The resource sharing takes place within the context of force sharing. How the force is applied creates a conduit through which the earth material and human capabilities get shaped to fit the pattern dictated by the force conduits, namely the force extensions. Humans constantly use the earth material as the basis for creating shared goods and services. Whether it is a loaf of bread, toilet paper, or an automobile, the earth material is processed into resources shared through exchanges with others.

The resource sharing is rarely one-sided, always made of humans giving and taking resources in different forms. It always seeks to reach a point of balance in what is given and taken. No different than force sharing, resource sharing becomes more complex in human interactions. In the same manner that humans have to manage force sharing to not expose anyone to brute force, they also have to manage resource sharing. It is obvious that no one should be left out of resource sharing. Those left out would be harmed in that they would not get the resources they need in life.

There is another key component in managing resource sharing. An inherent in-built human tendency "to take extra resources" when sharing resources. When sharing resources, every individual leans toward giving less and taking more. From the individual's point of view that is a good strategy. The taker ends at a better resource position. Everyone does this. This makes every human a "resource taker." Collectively, humans create a society of resource takers. Resource sharing originates, takes shape, and finalizes in a society of resource takers.

The human is both <u>force applier</u> and <u>resource taker</u>. Force and resource sharing manifest in a society of force appliers and resource takers. From force applier and resource taker we arrive at the human as "knowledge processor." As knowledge processors humans manage what they know or do not know. What the human knows is knowledge and that which is not known is ignorance. The human as knowledge processor is "converter of ignorance to knowledge." Knowledge (what we know) and ignorance (what we do not know) are interlinked permanently, only changing in proportion.

In managing the application of force and allocation of resources, humans must be both "ignorance managers" and "knowledge managers." In sharing force and resources, especially in the form of goods and services, ignorance and knowledge are interlinked. Through goods and services, humans constantly share knowledge and ignorance with each other. The management of knowledge and ignorance in human interactions is as challenging as management of force and resources.

When managing force, resources, knowledge, and ignorance every human assumes an inherent ability to set direction for others, direction as to how force, resources, and knowledge and ignorance are to be managed. "Direction setting" reflects the human uniqueness in the universe. Every human is a unique force applier, resource taker, and converter of ignorance to knowledge. Uniqueness brings the presumption of being as good if not better than others. That is why humans constantly set direction for one another and in doing so give rise to shared directions. No different than force sharing and resource sharing, life directions are also shared.

Humans fail in force sharing, fail in resource sharing, fail in knowledge sharing, and also fail in setting shared directions. The failure is the result of knowledge-giving deficiencies and the ignorance content inherent in anything humans make and use.

Without a common sharing direction, the result is often failed management of force, resources, and knowledge and ignorance, but nonetheless, the attempt at sharing continues. Whether parent directing the child or the boss directing the worker, humans constantly engage in acts of setting and responding to shared directions along dimensions of force, resources, and knowledge and ignorance.

These have been the foundational elements of the "societal sharing system," but a key question remains. If the sharing phenomenon is so foundational, so prevalent, why is the typical human so ignorant of the societal sharing system? This is a vexing question, a measure of human inability to manage knowledge and ignorance well. Let us dig deeper into the details.

Managing force societally

It is obvious that managing force, resources, knowledge, and direction setting is critical to humans creating and maintaining the societal sharing system. It originates at the elementary science of force and resources applicable to anything in the universe. Everything in human life and everything in the universe takes place within force fields. Everywhere on earth and in the universe, material structures held together by force move within force fields. There is no exception to this foundational condition. If there is an exception, at our current knowledge level we are incapable of seeing it. At our current level of knowledge we only see this: without exception, in order to exist, force has to be managed first.

Force management gives shape to the allocation of resources. Every material found relevant to human life is a "resource." The resource takes shape within the force fields. Every human is a force applier on earth material. Every human is a force applier on other humans. Since every human defines what a "resource" is and which resources are needed in life, when humans deal with each other societally, they collectively manage the application of force and allocation of resources for everyone.

How do humans manage force societally? In its most primal form, humans manage their lives according to the "direct use of brute force." This is like everyone carrying a spear, a sword, a gun, or some other weapon as means of settling affairs and interactions. Through direct use of brute force the human takes the needed resources. True, in doing so it harms others, but that is how brute force works. Brute force is the "harm thrower." Anyone exposed gets harmed. A society built on brute force is a "society of harm throwers." Harm-throwing is the only choice for humans when all they have to deal with one another is brute force.

Brute force, always, is the primal starting point. Can humans learn to avoid it? To reduce or perhaps even eliminate harm-throwing? For millennia humans have applied brute force and have known its results. Through experience they have learned brute force creates a destructive social structure. Worse, it always produces the lowest levels of goods and services. Those worrying about being exposed to the brute force of others rarely engage in acts of producing and distributing goods and services for others. From millennia of experience, getting harmed and getting little in goods and services, humans have learned about the design that moves the use of brute force into the background of human interactions. This has been a two-step process. Both steps have to be set up societally with no guarantee that it will work, but the alternative, the world of harm-throwers, is always a nightmare.

Humans have diligently worked on these two steps. The first step, share the brute force of all individuals and concentrate the shared force of the individuals into a societal one. The societal concentrated force is made available to every individual to serve the needs of every individual. Today we recognize such concentrated force as police and armed forces. The second step, extend the societal concentrated force to create the type of force humans can apply on one another without the ill effects of brute force. We are familiar with such "force extensions." They are the society's rules, laws, and regulations.

Here we face a historical dilemma. How can the makers and implementers of the two steps remain ignorant of what they have done or why they have done it? Yet that is the case. Ignorance of such ingenious force management technique is pervasive in every society on earth at all times. It is a historical shortcoming of the human mind, a shortcoming of social conditioning. The typical individual in human societies does not recognize the societal force management and force sharing that create the "extended force" out of the societal "concentrated force" in order to bring softness into human interactions. More important, they do not see that through it the society increases the possibilities for production and distribution of goods and services for daily human needs.

It is not that we cannot see the physical evidence of the societal concentrated force or the application of force extensions that emerge from it or the wonderful production and distribution of goods and services to satisfy everyone's daily needs. The goods and services are evident everywhere in the stores. In obvious physical form, the concentrated force also manifests as police and armed forces. The extended force governs everyone's life in the form of rules, laws, and regulations that the society's "force managers," namely the politicians and courts, create and maintain. Yet no one seems to see this wonderful human construct for managing brute force in the human individual's daily life. This is astounding, but I am not done. There is another troubling dimension to ignorance of how force is societally managed and why. The "force extension" may seem simple and straightforward, but it is not. Its creation and maintenance is completely dependent on the societal knowledge base and knowledge processing capabilities of the individuals that create the society. The force extension idea—ingenious, yet the force extensions are hard to create and maintain as the primary form of force management in human societies. The force extensions—rules, laws, and regulations originate at the societal concentrated force—a shared arrangement. Instead of brute force it allows humans to use extended force in directing and influencing one another's lives. Yet the ability to make and use force extensions is always suspect.

The extended force is an innovative device, yet its creation and use does not mean brute force disappears from human interactions.

To the contrary, the society's concentrated force is "brute force" ready to be applied. Moreover, there is always the possibility of the individual choosing to walk away from the extended force to use brute force. The society's concentrated force will counter and neutralize that individual, often by capturing and limiting that person's presence in the society—putting the individual in prison. The "prison" always signals the society's inability to manage brute force well.

The society's concentrated brute force always lurks in the background to counter anyone that fails to abide by the force extensions when dealing with other humans. Anyone that does not conduct his or her life according to the force extensions would have to manage it in brute force interactions with the police, and in the extreme, with the armed forces. We often refer to the extended force network backed by the societal concentrated force as the "rule of law." The extended force network is like a *suit of force extensions* everyone wears when interacting with others. The suit of force extensions replaces the sword and gun that humans use when interacting with one another through brute force.

I am often asked, why not continue to use words like law and police? Instead, why introduce new words like force extensions and concentrated force? The answer is simple. Words like law and police no longer provide a foundational view of the human managing force. In contrast, force extension and concentrated force directly inform of the force dimension and how we are managing it. That understanding is critical to better managing the human life, especially if we consider a divine source of knowledge, the Sermon on the Mount, as our way of living on the earth.

Managing the resources

The workplace is the major location where resources are shared. In its foundational form the workplace operates within the extended force network—the rule of law. It is characterized as a profit-making sharing system. It will take the resources of others in the process of providing goods and services that satisfy their daily needs. To understand the workplace we must first understand resource taking and its role in human life. Why should the extended force network allow resource taking in exchanges of goods and services? The answer is simple. Every human, by nature, is a "resource taker." Every human must take resources of the earth and others in order to satisfy what the person needs for daily life. No human would survive if he or she ceases to act as taker of resources of the earth and others. The extended force network, by purposeful design, directs the resource takers toward "voluntary exchanges of resources." If I need bread, the extended force network and the exchange-based resource taking allow me to get the bread. I voluntarily agree to the extra resource—the profit—the maker of bread takes from me. All goods and services come with their own profit tag—resources taken from others. In the voluntary exchanges we all agree to such measures of resource taking. Managing the "society of resource takers" is one of converting it into a "society of voluntary exchangers."

The built-in machinery of the human mind is not created for "even" exchanges with the earth and others. As resource taker no human is willing to engage in even exchanges; everyone wants to take more resources and give less in whatever one does. Those good at voluntary exchanges that satisfy the needs of others make a profit in each exchange. The profits accumulate to become a personal pile of resources. The profits earned—the resources taken—in voluntary exchanges add up and pile into "accumulated resources." This places tremendous individual and societal value on "accumulated resources." It is traditional to refer to accumulated resources with names like wealth and profit. The person that accumulates resources through production and exchange of goods and services owns and controls the accumulated resources. The accumulated resources become "wealth" for its creator. It is the design of the extended force network that allows the creation of wealth and defines the assignment of ownership. All these arrangements originate at how humans share force and resources.

Through millennia of experience humans have arrived

at the conclusion that they cannot manage force well without concentrating and extending it. They cannot manage resources well without allowing voluntary resource taking. Therefore the force and resource management in human societies become the "force-based resource taking system." It manifests as "exchange-based resource taking" at the level of daily life. The "force-based resource taking system" is the operating basis for force and resource management in every social arrangement humans have ever put together. It can exist in brute or extended force domains. When in the brute force domain, it produces little goods and services and harms a lot. When in the extended force domain, it produces lots of goods and services and harms little.

The exchange-based resource taking system does not use brute force in human interactions. It focuses on exchange-based production and distribution of goods and services, an arrangement in which every human is given the opportunity to take the resources of others for oneself through serving the needs of others. The resources taken from others turn into personal accumulated resources—things we know as wealth. The wealth is a byproduct of the method of force and resource management the society adopts to benefit all humans. It provides what humans need in daily life while eliminating or minimizing the use of destructive brute force on humans. This viable arrangement among interacting humans, created over thousands of years, is still imperfect and needs to improve.

The fact remains, however, the force-based resource taking system put together by any society is the best that a society can do with its societal knowledge base and the knowledge processing capabilities of its members. Is there an alternative to the force-based resource taking system? No. Is there any way that humans can cease to be force applier and resource taker? No. I see no such possibilities. The whole universe is defined by application of force and flow of resources, but there is always the human imagination of alternatives. The human mind is the creator of alternatives. Within the mind the human needs no external universe. It can create its own universe. Nonetheless, any alternative to the force-based resource taking system has to demonstrate that it can do better than the voluntary, exchange-based resource taking system set up in the extended force network. At the moment there are no contenders.

Rather, there are only variants of the force-based resource taking system. Such variations are most pronounced when comparing societies that do or do not know how to manage force well. Both the extended force network and the concentrated force are "human-made things." They suffer from human deficiencies in construction and maintenance of human-made things no different than anything else humans make and use. As a thing, the extended force network can be simple or complex, dismal or well-functioning. The concentrated force can be used to provide and maintain the force extensions, or deployed in confrontations with other centers of concentrated force where killing humans and destroying human societies would be the norm. But in all variations, the management fundamentals of extended and concentrated forces and the allocation of resources as goods and services remain the same. Humans must learn and manage those fundamentals well if societies are to remain stable and functional.

Then comes the individual. The individual must manage force and resources well when forming and maintaining the societal sharing system in which humans interact daily. Every production and exchange of goods and services involves the sharing of capabilities and resources among humans as well as the taking of resources from one another. Sharing and taking are inseparable, the sharing a form of the societal joining of human capabilities to amplify the production and distribution of goods and services humans need in daily life. Resource taking is the engine that powers the sharing process. It provides the impetus for the human to remain a participant in producing and distributing goods and services for others. It acts as the *measuring rod* for whether humans are efficient in production and distribution of goods and services, and whether what is produced and distributed corresponds to what humans need in daily life.

Any arrangement of human capabilities incapable of resource

taking—making no profit, making no one rich—signals it is either managed by incompetents or incapable of providing the goods and services humans want. Force-based resource taking and exchange-based resource taking are prevalent in every society. After millennia of societal life, humans know of no other way of managing force and resources. Anyone that bemoans the current human condition of profit making and the dominance of the rich must show an alternative to the force-based resource taking system. Otherwise, any complaint is merely pointing not at an alternative but either at deficiencies of the force-based resource taking system or at human ignorance of the force-based resource taking system. Pointing at deficiencies must organize humans toward understanding and reducing those deficiencies.

Wealth or fealth?

When not aware of emphasis placed by the divine on knowledge-giving deficiencies we become stuck in the current designs of the force-based resource taking system. We make sure we are aligned with the societal force network—obeying the rules and laws. We seek to take as much resources as we can from others at the lowest possible level of sharing our own capabilities with others. Let me share an extreme example. Of course not everyone does this but many would love to do it, especially when they hear the success stories of those that have done it. At the center of this example is the lack of knowledge of the societal sharing system. This knowledge deficiency is most obvious when humans seek to take the resources of others without giving anything in return. With that introduction I now give you the specifics of my example.

You buy a house for $100,000 with money borrowed from a bank at 5% interest rate. You keep the house for one year, paying the bank the interest of $5,000, then, at the end of the year, you sell the house for $300,000. You pay off the bank loan and gain the wealth of $200,000. Of the $200,000 you just gained you have spent almost none of your capabilities and resources. How did you create it? Simple, through speculative behavior that the resource takers find enticing and valuable. It is valuable because with your $200,000 you buy a house. Now you have a house that is yours. You have gained something for nothing. It cost you only $5,000 in interest payments to get the $200,000 house. The capabilities and resources spent on getting the house—the $5,000 paid as interest—are much less than the capabilities and resources gone into building the $200,000 house. On your own, if you had $5,000 the most you could do is to get a used car or a two-week vacation in Europe. Then, how did you manage to get a house worth $200,000 with your $5,000?

You did so through the pursuit of <u>fake wealth</u>. I call fake wealth "fealth," another new word. What is the difference between fealth and wealth? At first glance, nothing. Whether you save $200,000 after working hard for two decades or play in the speculative real estate market by borrowing resources from a bank, buying a house, waiting for the price to double or triple in a short time, and then selling it to gain the same $200,000, the end point is the same. In both cases you end with $200,000 in the bank. If so, why call one wealth and the other fealth? Isn't the only difference between the two the degree of ease or difficulty of getting it? Why shouldn't every human try to get the easy wealth if one can? The outcome is the same, not the starting base. In one the base is made of hard work for decades, in the other no hard work and only a short time.

If I am giving them different names, implying one is real and the other fake, then I am seeing them different even though they are both the same bundle of wealth. In fact, while the society has little if any problem with wealth, it faces a serious problem with fealth. The society cannot sustain a resource taking structure based on fealth. Fealth takes real goods and services without having given anything in return. It is a one-sided deal. It is not *like* stealing, it *is* stealing.

In the societal sharing system it is not possible to adopt a resource taking structure where one takes real goods and services created with shared capabilities of others without offering an equivalent in return. In the game of creating fealth only a small group get to convert their fealth into wealth in the form of goods and services. They benefit from doing so by gaining something for nothing, the ideal of every resource taker. But the speculative prices that create fealth eventually cannot be sustained. Eventually the societal sharing system cannot bear the burden of exchanging fealth for wealth. The society's resource taking processes and the production and distribution of goods and services collapse.

What is intriguing is that after collapse, the fealth that has not been converted to wealth becomes worthless. Consider the house that started at the price of $100,000. I might be the last person that bought it for $600,000, hoping to sell it for $1.2 million. But after collapse I am stuck with the $1.2 million fealth-priced house and have to face the fact of wealth-making. After collapse of the fealth-driven market no one is capable of paying more than $100,000 for the house because that is its value in terms of wealth, in terms of the shared capabilities that created it. The $600,000 which I borrowed for the house was actually made of $100,000 of human capabilities and resources to produce the house and $500,000 of speculative expectations for which little or no human capabilities were spent.

The two, real capabilities and speculative expectations, combined to create fealth. If only a few humans played the fealth-creation game, no different than the few that choose to become thieves and robbers to take the resources of others through brute force, then the societal sharing system stability would not be affected. Now imagine it is not a handful of humans creating fealth but everyone is trying to do it. Everyone is buying a house in the hope and expectation that in a year or two it will be sold for double or triple the amount borrowed. The society cannot sustain such resource taking structure where everyone puts little into creation of what the humans need but gets much in return.

At some point of fealth creation, the amount of fealth entering the societal sharing system becomes so large that exchanges of real goods and services become impossible. The house that was built using $100,000 of human capabilities, after four cycles of fealth is now selling at $1 million. Humans are still clamoring to borrow resources to buy it in the hope that it would soon sell for $3 million. The justification for such behavior is the success stories from the previous fealth creators. We can point at the one that bought at $100,000 and sold at $300,000, or the one that bought at $300,000 and sold at $600,000. This illusion of creating something out of nothing benefits few, but harms all. Can the force-based resource taking system address this serious problem? Can it create force extensions that seriously punish any such behavior? The answer is no. Why? Because in its initial stages, it is very easy to hide the speculative pursuit of fealth in the normal price movements caused by supply and demand. Moreover, it is a game that can be played with any of the goods and services humans make and use in life.

The origin of fealth's value is at the value of "wealth." There is too much power in wealth that amplifies human capabilities. I might be one of the best professors, one of the hardest working, but even after decades of work I cannot put together the wealth that will get me a villa in the south of France. Yet I can get the same villa in a matter of a couple of years if I play the fealth game well in a product that attracts price speculation.

If I were religious I may call fealth the "stuff of the fallen." Not being religious, I tend to see it as resource takers gone berserk. They seek to create and convert fealth to wealth while totally ignorant of the adverse impact on the societal sharing system that sustains us all. Such fealth-focused ignorance amplifies and develops into means of mass destruction, means of bringing down the whole society. The fealth creation always ends in societal collapse. At the point of collapse the market can no longer sustain the fealth-amplified prices. The ones that borrowed $1 million in the hope they will sell next year at $3 million come to the realization that no one is capable of paying them $3 million. They then realize their own capabilities cannot even pay the $50,000 annual interest on $1 million borrowed. The fealth-amplified prices return to the level based on exchange of human capabilities. The bank that lent $1 million has no money of its own, it is lending the money of the depositors. So when it forecloses on the $1M house and can only get $200,000 in selling the house, the masses have lost $800,000. The bank on its own is bankrupt and if the government is to bail out the bank, it is taking the money from the taxpayers to save the depositors. At the final count everyone in the society is losing in the fealth-based collapse. All lament that the social sharing system has become dysfunctional; one cannot sell yesterday's $1 million house for even $200,000. This is the lament of the resource takers suffering in the aftereffects of fealth creation. Ignorant of what they have done, they cannot see the pain they have inflicted not only on themselves but on the whole society by playing the fealth game. So let me conclude that humans are badly stuck in knowledge-giving deficiencies about wealth-making. Can the Sermon on the Mount address this behavior, the human as fealth-seeker?

Here is a test. What have you learned from the fourth beatitude that applies to the fealth-seeking problem? Don't read anymore and think. After thinking, continue to read. First, fealth is an imbalance, thus an injustice. The fourth beatitude tells us to continually and diligently remain focused on justice, on maintaining the "balance" in the societal sharing system. Yet in creation and use of fealth everyone remains blind to what is happening until the society collapses. Then there is the moaning and groaning by all that feel the injustice. If everyone continually remained focused on the fealth injustice, it would not be allowed to come into existence and grow. The real estate agents would not exponentially increase the house prices. The banks would not lend to buyers whose sole purpose is to benefit from fealth. But that is much easier said than practiced, especially by those that benefit from fealth.

We have to pay serious attention to managing the societal sharing system, especially the virus of fealth which infects the societal sharing system where a small group seeks to become wealthy overnight at the expense of collapsing and harming the whole society. The societal sharing system thrives on activities that serve the daily needs of humans. It thrives on reducing the ignorance content in human interactions and exchanges. In contrast, fealth is ignorance-filled resource-taking-mesmerized activity that allows some humans to take substantial amounts of resources from others without giving any of their own in return. They are thieves that use the societal sharing system in their act of thieving. Its outcome no different than pointing a gun at others, taking their resources. Yet, since it is done within the extended force network and through voluntary market transactions, it satisfies the societal norms for resource taking. No different than application of brute force to take the resources of others, however, it eventually causes the society's exchange-based resource taking processes to collapse. It inflicts substantial harm on many.

No society survives when its members play the game of taking a lot and giving nothing or little in return. So what do we do? Remember the first step, the first beatitude, and focus on knowledge-giving deficiencies. Fealth originates at one of the biggest knowledge deficiencies, not seeing the societal sharing system as sustainer of all. Everyone should engage in knowledge seeking and knowledge sharing to identify and eliminate fealth. Since fealth is the biggest hidden form of injustice, it must be on everyone's mind when in pursuit of justice. It requires constant unwavering attention by everyone to maintain justice. Fealth cannot be left invisible. The injustice of fake wealth must be address by everyone in every moment of life.

Playing with models of justice, made by humans

It is easy to point at fealth and identify it as a serious case of societal injustice, a destroyer of societal balance, but the question of justice involves the whole societal sharing system and is bigger than fealth. In the fourth step, the fourth beatitude, we are asked if we can intently and continuously act in accordance with "justice." This is both a capability question and a choice-making question. Outside of diligent attention, the task of filling the suitcase of the word justice is left to us. How would we fill that suitcase? How are we capable of filling it?

Given that every human is unique in the universe, we face the challenge of aligning the uniqueness of many to arrive at the many-agree position on "justice." Facing uniqueness, we have to manage the differences and differentials among humans and as such cannot point at a single recipe for "justice;" never a single design that can be applied to every human. The divine knows this and that is why we are only taught to hunger and thirst after justice, constantly focusing on maintaining the societal balance whatever that might be. In the fourth beatitude we are told nothing more about justice, what it is and how it can be managed. All that is left to the human. We have arrived at "justice" after navigating the first three steps, the first three beatitudes. Is that important? Is there a message in the sequence through which we have arrived at "justice?" It is clear that a society that does not manage knowledge-giving deficiency and mourning situations well and cannot assess its alternatives patiently and nonviolently, will not be able to set up a just structure to manage differences and differentials among humans. Justice cannot be the first step, cannot be the first among the beatitudes—it is the last step, achieving the balance of force and resources after excelling in knowledge processing.

From what we know now, the question of justice has been left to us. Throughout history humans have always sensed the need for societal balance in human interactions and have tried to reach it through the word "justice." In its barest view justice is a "thing" humans make and use. Starting with the force-based resource taking system, the application of force and allocation of resources are all about organizing the human capabilities and applying the human capabilities to what all humans need in daily life. From this picture the word "justice" implies "balance" in organizing the human capabilities to serve the human needs. The deviations from the point of balance would be "injustice," imbalances that harm the human.

Let us think operationally and ask where does the society manage the collective of human capabilities? Since capabilities always aggregate as many-agree positions, where does the society manage its many-agree positions? In the modern setting the societal management of many-agree positions happens primarily in assemblies we know as the House of Representatives and the Senate. There, the many-agree positions find representation and seek to become the society's all-agree positions. How do those managing the many-agree positions in the House of Representatives and the Senate reach a point of balance we can call justice? At this time they primarily do so through using brute force. The formula for force-based justice is simple. They all have accepted that the many-agree position that reaches 51% is "just" at using brute force to declare itself "all-agree" to make the remaining 49% align with the 51% position. It is a force-based way of defining and enforcing justice, yet a form of justice that continually invites retaliation. Those forced to follow the many-agree way of today's 51% seek to become tomorrow's 51% and apply brute force on those that previously had done the same. This is a game of applying brute force on each other's many-agree positions, a battleground of many-agree positions in which the brute force is the arbiter, with the potential to eventually destroy the society in force-based confrontations of many-agree positions. Even though this form of "justice" is most dysfunctional in the long run, today, given the human capabilities, it is the only way human societies know when reaching for justice.

Even when we see justice as the balanced application of human capabilities to satisfy daily human needs within the context of many-agree positions that have been "justly" declared all-agree, the picture remains vague. The battle of 51% positions is never-ending, no one winning decisively. The continuing battle of 51% positions is the best evidence that there are many ways of filling the suitcase of the word justice. Each group does it differently and the challenge of defining the balanced human life remains unending. Let us assume this observation is true and let us step beyond the justice defined by battle of 51-percenters to sample the ways of others that have thought about justice. [39]

The first that we visit is the utilitarian approach to justice. In the force-based resource taking system, it sees justice as an arrangement that produces the greatest level of societal happiness. The target of justice: happiness. Is this not the same as trading one suitcase word for another? Instead of seeking justice we now seek happiness. So long as one is "happy" with the management of force and resources, one assumes life is in balance and justice served. Assume it works, at least for most, screwing only the few. So long as most humans are happy, the utilitarian justice has no concern with the few unhappy ones. Here, at the start, we run into the problem of injustice to the few. Even for the most we face the problem of not knowing what the suitcase word "happiness" means, no different than not knowing "justice." Both happiness and justice come with big, empty suitcases. Replacing one suitcase word with another does not mean higher knowledge content, it only means "playing with suitcase words."

Think of the beatitudes where the divine knowledge is a choice. We are told we would be happy if we choose to use it, but clearly some will choose not to use it and would remain less happy. In such setting life becomes a mix of happy and less happy. Is that the same as the utilitarian view of justice? The utilitarian view has replaced the word "justice" with the word "happiness" and wants to make and use a lot of things that make people happy, thus making the world just. It is ironic that this is no different than wanting a lot of justice and only wishing occasional injustice. In all this another fact stares the human in the face. In the beatitudes the mix of happy and not happy is a human choice, but such is not the case in the utilitarian model. The unhappy ones do not choose to become unhappy. It is the chosen design of the societal sharing system that makes them unhappy. Are we now stuck with understanding the difference between choosing and not choosing? Can we, or do we, have the knowledge to resolve the paradox?

Let's have a look at another form of justice. This one does not talk about happiness; instead it equates justice with fairness. "Fairness" is a suitcase word. How should we fill the suitcase of fairness? Consider John Rawls as the one filling the suitcase. He has developed a fairness model of justice where he defines "fairness" as principles chosen by those that do not know their position in the societal sharing system. It seems simple and straightforward. If I am given the task of designing the society's system of justice AND I do not know whether I will be rich or poor, occupy the position of worker or corporate executive, would I design the system of justice fairly because I don't know where I would end up? That sounds like the ignorant deciding justice. Or is it?

John Rawls argues that under such circumstances humans would tend to choose the principle of "equal liberty" and the principle of "allowing social and economic inequalities so long as the inequalities improve and protect the society's least advantaged." On the surface this has a "mourning situation" focus. Those facing the mourning situation are labeled "the least advantaged." This system of justice manages the force-based resource taking system such that the condition of those in the mourning situation improves, even though the condition of others might worsen. Note that there is no attempt at removing the mourning situation. All this form of justice wants is not to have the mourning situation get worse. I don't know much about this method of seeking justice and have to think about whether it provides societal balance. For now, let us direct our thinking to the suitcase words this system of justice uses. Instead of "happiness," we are dealing with "liberty" and "least advantaged" as definers of "fairness" that creates justice. The challenge of dealing with the suitcase words remains. On top of that, it is impossible to find those humans that know nothing about the outcomes of choice-making among humans. It is those individuals that would decide the fairness principles.

Assume we find an individual that knows nothing about the outcomes of choice-making among humans. How would that individual's ideas transform into the society's many-agree force-backed positions that would dictate the way of life for everyone? That is a huge force management problem. What if for everyone the principles pronounced by that individual are nothing but few-agree positions? All of this returns to the point that we do not know what justice is and have a hard time deciding what it will be. Yet as balance of life, it is critical that we achieve justice.

So far we have sampled two views, the utilitarian and fairness models. They do not rely on religious concepts. How would justice change if we add a religious twist? As an example, consider the Catholic Church's view of justice. It is similar to the Rawlsian model but instead of the "least advantaged" it uses the word "poor." In the Catholic design those with better resource positions become responsible for managing the poor. Unlike Rawls who designs justice from the point of view of humans that do not know their position in the societal sharing system, the Church argues that it can design the society's system of justice because *it knows* the position of every human.

In the "I know you" system of justice, the suitcase word that the Catholic Church uses is "dignity." Every human is declared equal in dignity. With "dignity" being a suitcase word, how are we to fill it? This is how the Catholic Church fills it. In its view of justice, dignity is "having been created in the image of God." The utilitarian view jumped from justice to happiness. The Rawlsian view jumped from justice to fairness in dealing with the least advantaged. The Catholic Church jumps from justice to dignity and from there a bigger jump to "image of God" when dealing with the poor, the image of God being a really large suitcase.

At this point let me stop to talk about something even more important. I observe that none of the justice systems we have sampled are about "justice," the societal balance in human interactions. Instead they are more about the suitcase words that represent knowledge deficiencies and mourning situations. All deficiencies are points of unhappiness. The happiness model wants humans to address the knowledge deficiencies in order to remove or at least minimize the unhappiness. The least advantaged and the poor are indicators of existing or potential mourning situations, extreme cases of knowledge deficiencies. In the Sermon on the Mount the human as knowledge giver sets the scene. The poor and disadvantaged are not identified as groups of humans needing attention. Instead the human is described as "knowledge giver" and "mourning-remover." It is only in the fourth step, the fourth beatitude, that the human, having performed as knowledge-giver and mourning-remover, becomes capable of reaching the point of balance in the force-based resource taking system and sets the foundation for movement toward justice as balancing the human differences and differentials.

We have only sampled a few views of justice, yet they demonstrate the variety of human thought about the just way of managing differences and differentials in human societies. In the Sermon on the Mount, the fourth beatitude leaves justice to human. The message is clear; humans cannot address justice until they excel in walking the path set up by the first three beatitudes. Unless humans focus on knowledge seeking, knowledge sharing, addressing mourning situations, and assessing alternatives patiently without reliance on brute force, they would not be able to determine what justice means for the human individual and the human societies. That is the divine way of reaching justice. The justice models originating at utilitarian, Rawlsian, Catholic Church, or 51-percenter views rely on human wisdom. We cannot dismiss any of these models because justice will always rely on human wisdom. That is the divine message. But to reach a high level of wisdom, the human would choose to walk the first three steps. That is also a divine message of choice. Walking the four steps, or not, what is the difference? Where would the difference be most evident?

The outcome of not paying attention to knowledge giving and mourning situations becomes most evident in lack of preparedness for the "big" mourning situation of eschaton, the earth crossing the swarm of cometary fragments. The beatitudes are quite clear, while we have a choice at following them or not, if we choose to follow them we would be happy especially at the time when the earth changes radically.

Hungering and thirsting ... What!

If justice as point of balance of force-based resource taking is to be determined by humans, if the divine is not going to tell us about the ideal structure of justice, what is the point of thirsting and hungering after it? What is going on here? For years I wondered why the human must "hunger and thirst after righteousness." After the knowledge deficiencies are addressed, the mourning situations taken care of, and humans are patient and gentle in assessing and choosing alternatives, why not also follow the patient path toward justice? If humans do the first three beatitudes, the fourth should require little in maintaining "justice" as point of balance in application of force and allocation of resources.

Then I had a small but eye-opening experience. It demonstrated what happens when no one is thirsting and hungering for justice in human interactions. The experience itself, quite minor, a situation of mileage reimbursement. It started with the observation that no one had told me about mileage reimbursement and I learned of it after ten years. I was displeased, the only person excluded from getting mileage. I saw it as an injustice that had to be corrected. But in seeking justice I quickly learned the eye-opening lesson. If justice is not managed in current time and injustice is allowed to propagate, it is difficult to go back and correct the injustices of the past. Here is how the pursuit of mileage justice unfolded.

In the search to address the mileage injustice, the boss took the position that he had the vague memory that I had declared I do not want to receive mileage reimbursement, therefore my exclusion was just because I had agreed to that injustice. Widening the search for justice brought in the person in charge of the Human Resources Department. He indicated that the organization is under budget pressure and not willing to go back ten years, but might consider going back one to two years, providing partial justice for settlement of injustice. Furthermore, the HR manager took the position that the proof of injustice was my problem, not his. I was the one that had to come up with mileage information for the past ten years as he had no time or resources to spend on correcting the injustice of the past.

Hmm, thirsting and hungering for justice, by everyone, no exceptions, now I could see it. If my colleagues, everyone at the HR department, everyone at the organization, thirsted and hungered after justice, in the first month someone would have noticed that by not filing mileage reimbursement I was creating a situation of injustice. My boss would have noticed that everyone but me is receiving it, the HR department would have recognized that for some reason I am excluded from mileage reimbursement, and my colleagues would have asked if I am getting reimbursed for mileage. I and everyone else would have returned to point of balance if everyone in organization thirsted and hungered for justice. Yet none of that happened because no one, including myself, was thirsting and hungering for justice.

Without current focus on justice, without everyone thirsting and hungering for justice now, the injustice takes shape and accumulates. The pile of injustice grows and grows. Even when someone eventually notices, it cannot be addressed or is very hard to address, if not impossible. Look at any other case of accumulated injustice. We cannot go back and address the injustice of enslaving a group of people or killing and torturing other people. The justice and injustice are best addressed in the present, when human acts. Thus the emphasis of the fourth beatitude on everyone hungering and thirsting to fairly manage the application of force and flow of resources. Is that easy? Clearly not, just look at the step at which it appears. The individual, group, and society must be current in balancing force and resources, or the imbalances accumulate.

In my mileage reimbursement experience I encountered another important observation. Now that I am aware of mileage reimbursement, the boss knows it and the HR Department knows it, I feel quite resistant asking for mileage reimbursement. I am doing the driving eligible for reimbursement, but feel extremely resistant to report it for reimbursement. It feels as if by getting reimbursed for current miles I am putting a seal of approval on past injustices. It is an odd feeling, yet it is quite strong. This reminds me of my observation that in my classes most black students are resistant to excel in learning. For decades and centuries they were not allowed to engage in learning. Now, allowed, they have no intention of doing so. I now understand that behavior, the type of resistance that does not want to put the seal of approval on injustices of the past.

I know that by not reporting the mileage, by not getting reimbursed, I lose money. By not studying hard and excelling academically my black student would also lose money by not preparing to land good careers and jobs. Still, the injustice of the past hangs like a weight that cannot be discarded. It drags one down, does not allow one to rise to the surface and it hurts. Yet such suffering is a form of personal protest to injustice of the past, the injustice that has not been or cannot be addressed. This further highlights the demand by the fourth step, the fourth beatitude, on everyone that has chosen to follow the Sermon on the Mount to thirst and hunger for justice. It is the only way the individual and society can be relieved from the deadweight of injustices piled up in the past and continuing into the future.

VII

Ahh, Being Tested, by the Divine

The Sermon on the Mount does not throw away the force-based resource taking system nor can it. The application of force, allocation of resources, and conversion of ignorance to knowledge are foundational aspects of human existence. They cannot be eliminated, but can they be managed differently, ideally in a way that moves the human toward perfection in individual and societal life where no one is harmed and everyone receives everything one needs through sharing of capabilities with others?

The beatitudes are divine knowledge. How do we demonstrate that we have learned it? The answer, take a test. Why take a test? We're adults, not kids. After all, what are the beatitudes, eight verses? Only four verses on today's test. What's the big deal? In that earthly logic, we are forgetting that we are dealing with divine knowledge. The test would show whether we are morons, meaning, incapable of high levels of knowledge processing, or have advanced to the level of comprehending what the divine says.

The test is a measure of the degree of alignment with the divine knowledge and shows purposefulness. The divine doesn't just teach, the divine tests to ensure we have learned.

Having learned how to approach the four operational steps, the four beatitudes, we are now ready to demonstrate the degree of our understanding of what the divine has taught in the beatitudes. Like any professor in human societies, the divine "tests us" to make sure we have understood the teaching. Then, after succeeding in the test, the divine improves our competence by applying what we have learned to various real life situations. In today's jargon, the real-life applications are called "case studies." If we pass the tests and demonstrate competence in analysis of the case studies, we will be declared ready to apply what we have learned in the real world and share our capabilities in ways that transform the world from current force-based ways to the knowledge-based way of the Sermon on the Mount.

The four steps, the four beatitudes, are like classrooms. When we do well in the first step, the first class, we are promoted to the second step, the second class. When we do well there, we move up to the next class. If we do not do well in any class, we return back to the previous class. If really bad, we return to the first step, the first class, then repeat the learning process from the beginning. When we move down, we have not failed, we just need to learn more at a previous step.

Back to the tests. They check what we have learned in each step, each classroom. If we fail in the tests, it is not time to do case studies. We need to get back to the classroom, do more knowledge seeking and knowledge sharing, and engage in deeper learning in each of the four steps. Then take the tests again. Once the tests are taken successfully, it is forward to analyzing the case studies. We move back and forth until eventually demonstrating the readiness to move into the world to transform it.

The design of the tests

Before we talk about the tests let us review what we know about the human. In the beatitudes the human is declared a "choice maker." If the human chooses the way of the divine he or she will be happy and best prepared to face the canopied earth—the kingdom of heaven—when it arrives. Before the tests, in the part of the Sermon on the Mount that the traditionalists call the "hermeneutical principles," the principles of managing knowledge bases and engaging in knowledge processing are addressed and the human is declared a "knowledge processor." When taking the test the human stands as choice maker and knowledge processor. The test offers an array of choices already made, knowledge processing already done, choices to be made, and knowledge processing to be made, all alternatives the test places before the human.

Let us take a step back and observe that the traditional view of the Sermon on the Mount never comes this far. It never sees the tests because it never sees the divine knowledge being offered in the beatitudes. The traditional view is confused; it lacks the knowledge processing capabilities to understand the divine knowledge. To the traditional view the test is nothing but a jumbled gathering of words. But we are not confused. We know the divine knowledge. We know we are being tested. So let us start with understanding the design of the tests.

There are six tests, each in multiple-choice format. The general outline of each multiple-choice test is simple:

It is said:	a) statement given
I say:	b) statement given
	c) statement given
	d) statement given
Implicit	e) statement not given

As a multiple-choice test this format looks both familiar and unfamiliar. It is familiar in the sense of being given a certain number of choices. It is unfamiliar in that a choice is missing from the test. It is kept out. Later we will see that it is the "obvious choice" that is kept out. This is like all the choices in the test being wrong and the correct choice like "none of the above" not being listed. The correct choice is assumed to be obvious and known implicitly. Hmm, that makes the test a bit tougher. Why would one of the multiple choices be left out? Because it is the obvious answer. If the "obvious answer" is given, then all other test items become irrelevant. One sees the obvious and chooses it. So, the test leaves the obvious out. The one taking the test has to analyze the multiple choices then reach the conclusion on the obvious answer not included in the test. That makes the test tough, not the usual multiple-choice test. But then again, the divine is not your usual teacher.

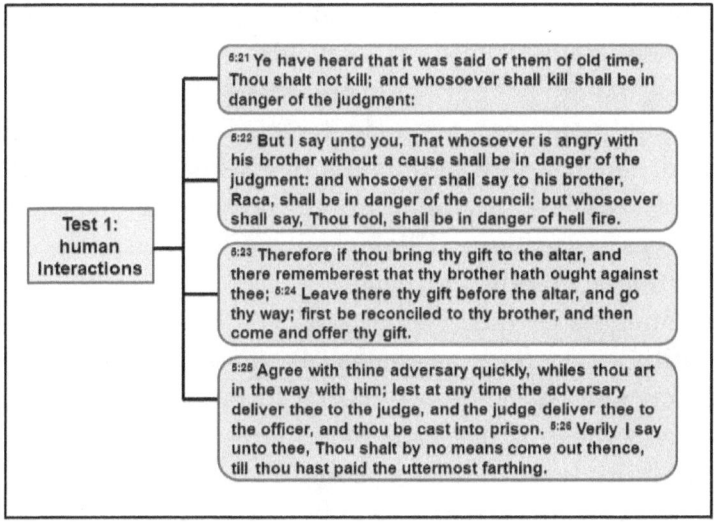

Okay, let us consider the first of the six tests. I will consider all of them in a separate book, here I focus only on the first test. The first multiple-choice test has four parts, all focused on human interactions. In the usual way of taking a multiple-choice test, we will consider and analyze each part separately in order to determine whether it is the correct one. We all know the method, we have all taken multiple-choice tests, though none were on divine knowledge and none were given by the divine.

Since the test is on the divine knowledge learned in the four beatitudes, each part in the multiple-choice test has to be considered in light of that knowledge. Okay, let us start answering the test. Let us focus on the first part in the multiple-choice test. It says:

> 5: 21 Ye have heard that it was said of them of old
> time, Thou shalt not kill; and whosoever shall
> kill shall be in danger of the judgment.

We have seen this before. Killing—killing a human—is the worst brute force application in human interactions. How do we address it, how do we manage it, how do we prevent it? Just saying "do not kill" would not create a good force management system. We have not seen brute force explicitly in any of the first two beatitudes, though it is implicitly present in some of the mourning situations. Brute force shows up in the third and fourth beatitudes. It is managed through gentleness of alternatives and diligent pursuit of "balance" in application of brute force and allocation of resources, a gentle and balanced design of the force-based resource taking system.

The analysis of the "do not kill" command starts with the first beatitude. The focus of analysis is on addressing knowledge-giving deficiencies. The most glaring form of knowledge-giving deficiency is the one that leads to humans killing humans. From the first beatitude we know we should recognize the "knowledge-giving deficiencies" and counter them with knowledge seeking and knowledge sharing. The first part of the test threatens the killer with being killed, turning it into a game of throwing "knowledge-giving deficiencies" at one another and not resolving them through knowledge seeking and knowledge sharing. That is not acceptable. The first beatitude is not about the battleground of knowledge-giving deficiencies using brute force as arbiter. It is about knowledge seeking and knowledge sharing to address and remove the knowledge deficiencies.

From the first beatitude we move to the second beatitude to see the "killing" as a "mourning situation" emerging from the lowest level of "knowledge giving" in human interactions, leading to application of brute force on humans, destroying humans. Every mourning situation always points to the crumbling foundation below, namely the deficiencies in knowledge seeking and knowledge sharing. Here again, the "do not kill or you will be killed" continues instead of resolving the mourning situation. This part of the test, rather than addressing the knowledge-giving deficiencies creates a *reciprocity* of "not killing" or a *reciprocity* of "being killed after killing others." It is a solution that always remains in the brute force domain. From the point of view of the divine knowledge in the beatitudes it would not be the correct choice. It seeks to create a *stalemate situation* in human killing than addressing the knowledge-giving deficiencies that give rise to humans killing humans. The first part in the multiple-choice test is out, the divine knowledge in the four beatitudes dismisses it. We move on.

Consider the second part in the multiple-choice test. It says:

> 5: 22 But I say unto you, That whosoever is angry with his brother without a cause shall be in danger of the judgment: and whosoever shall say to his brother, Raca, shall be in danger of the council: but whosoever shall say, Thou fool, shall be in danger of hell fire.

In analyzing this part in the multiple-choice test we start with the first beatitude and ask in human interactions what is the first human aspect we should consider. What can be the simplest, most elemental form of human behavior signaling "knowledge-giving deficiency"? The answer: anger. Whenever humans face knowledge-giving deficiency, whether it is originating at self or others, it causes anger. As the anger becomes more intense, the level of knowledge-giving deficiency arrives at the solution of exposing humans to brute force, the brute force that harms the human and destroys resources.

When I feel my boss does not recognize the value of my work (boss's knowledge deficiency), I get angry at the presence of such knowledge deficiency. My anger increases when I recognize I am not getting promoted (loss of resources). The boss notices my dissatisfaction, raises his voice and threatens my employment in the company (exposure to economic death, the brute force throwing me out of the workplace). This makes me really angry. In this interaction there is no attempt at addressing the knowledge deficiencies or improving the knowledge giving. It only amplifies the presence and accumulation of knowledge-giving deficiencies.

"Anger," felt anywhere, by anyone, signals the presence of knowledge-giving deficiency and the associated exposure to brute force and resource losses. The angry one feels the knowledge-giving deficiency but is not aware of the need to remove that knowledge-giving deficiency. Instead, the human feels a strong tendency to resort to brute force as a physical method of expressing anger. How is the human to manage "anger"? What about using brute force? In this part of the test we are told to manage anger by scaring the angry one into submission. Threatening the angry human with the worldly brute force directed by the council, and of course, the ultimate heavenly threat of hellfire. The second part of the test is a "brute force management" recipe that involves no knowledge seeking and knowledge sharing to address and remove the knowledge-giving deficiencies that create the anger. In the test, is this the right answer to choose? Clearly not.

Armed with the divine knowledge we know when we see anger we must recognize it as "knowledge-giving deficiency." The solution to anger—the solution to knowledge-giving deficiency—is through knowledge seeking and knowledge sharing. This part of the test does not consider the knowledge-based approach to human life and instead suggests reliance on brute force at both the human and divine levels. In comparison to the first part of the test, where the focus is on "killing reciprocity," in the second part of the test we are dealing with a lower degree of knowledge-giving deficiency. The knowledge-giving deficiency is not big enough to make humans kill one another but sufficiently big to make one angry to think about killing the other.

Why should we consider "anger" as a sign of knowledge-giving deficiency to be addressed and removed? To address any knowledge-giving deficiency takes time and resources. Instead of correcting and addressing the knowledge-giving deficiency, is it not easier to simply take the position that anger does not exist or should not exist or that it can be suppressed and made invisible? If somehow we remove or suppress anger, there would be no more need for knowledge seeking and knowledge processing. That sounds efficient but such removal or suppression is not possible because at the anger's core sits the knowledge-giving deficiency. That is why the second part of test cannot address anger through removal of anger, but seeks to suppress it through threat of brute force, whether that of the human or the divine. If I am threatened with brute force rather than being given knowledge, should I abandon knowledge seeking and knowledge sharing as way of addressing anger and go with brute force as way of suppressing anger and managing human life? That approach does not fit either the first beatitude or the third. In the first beatitude the focus remains on removing the knowledge-giving deficiencies and in the third beatitude on "gentle" and not force-based alternatives.

It is also important to note that "anger" is a few-agree, high-ignorance-content emotional position. It reeks with knowledge-giving deficiencies. It highlights serious knowledge-giving deficiencies in human interactions. Finding a force-based solution that bans anger would not be aligned with the beatitudes and therefore not the correct choice in the test. We move on and continue taking the test.

Consider the third part in the multiple-choice test. It says:

> 5:23 Therefore if thou bring thy gift to the altar, and there rememberest that thy brother hath ought against thee;

> [5:24] Leave there thy gift before the altar, and go thy
> way; first be reconciled to thy brother, and then
> come and offer thy gift.

In this part of the test we face a dilemma, the management of contradictions. If we are angry, sensing knowledge-giving deficiency, can the knowledge-based resolution come through conspicuous violations of the society's many-agree positions and force extensions? In the test the many-agree positions and force extensions are symbolized by the temple rituals. Such violations would be seen by others and cause concern as severe cases of knowledge-giving deficiency. How can an individual lack the knowledge to align oneself with society's many-agree positions and force extensions? That could make many angry.

Is it proper to take care of one's personal knowledge-giving deficiency, one's situation of anger, by exhibiting more knowledge-giving deficiencies and making many others angry? The hasty departure from established ways of knowledge processing does not justify the acts of knowledge seeking and knowledge sharing that address a minor knowledge-giving deficiency, perceived or actual. Tearing down the society's knowledge-packets, creating immense knowledge-giving deficiencies in order to remove a much smaller knowledge-giving deficiency, expands rather than reduces knowledge-giving deficiencies. It might even turn a small deficiency into a mourning situation.

Thus, in this multiple-choice test, the third part is not the correct choice. Breaking and violating many-agree positions and force extension for minor knowledge-giving deficiencies would not correspond to gains in knowledge seeking and knowledge sharing. It only invites greater possibilities of anger and brute force in face of knowledge-giving deficiencies that such action generates. Such behavior, if adopted societally, will quickly spiral out of control and cause many more possibilities of anger followed by spiraling application of brute force on humans. Such outcome is the opposite of the divine knowledge given in the beatitudes.

So far we have checked three parts of the multiple-choice test.

Do we see a pattern? Killing. Anger. Bother. A pattern is emerging. The choices we face in the test are designed to move down a high-to-low scale of knowledge-giving deficiencies in human interactions. In the first part of the test we saw the mourning situation of "killing," a situation in dire need of knowledge processing to address serious knowledge-giving deficiencies in human interactions, the type of deficiencies that give rise to human destruction. In the second part of the test we faced "anger" and the offer of a force-based solution for its eradication, thus ignoring the knowledge-giving deficiencies that gives rise to anger. When knowledge-giving deficiency is not addressed, allowed to remain and intensify, it has the potential to develop into mourning situations.

Moving below anger to things like annoyances, where does one draw the line for immediate action on knowledge-giving deficiency? In the third part of the test we face the rather vaguely described situation in which the individual *feels* something is not right in relation to someone. Having become aware that something might not be right, should the individual continue with the routine organizational activities (all acts of knowledge processing) or should one drop everything and rush to address the perceived knowledge-giving deficiency first and then return to performing the organizational routines? All deviant behaviors signal the presence of serious knowledge-giving deficiencies. Is "rushing" to address minor knowledge-giving deficiencies the proper way? More importantly, is violating the established positions, thus creating more knowledge-giving deficiencies justified when rushing to address minor knowledge-giving deficiencies?

If I am working on a factory's assembly line and remember I forgot to wash the dishes which will annoy my wife, should I drop whatever I am doing on the factory's assembly line and run to the house to wash the dishes, then return to take care of what I do on the assembly line? Would that stop the whole assembly line? Reduce the production and distribution of goods and services? Make many angry? The third beatitude tells us, having taken care of the mourning situations and having addressed the major and important anger-causing knowledge-giving deficiencies, it is time for patient and gentle knowledge processing among alternatives. Given the alternative of dropping everything to go and take care of a perceived annoyance or continuing to do what needs to be done now and later address the perceived annoyance, which one are we to choose?

The answer clearly lies in the fact that the societal and organizational knowledge processing has to continue and not be interrupted by observations of minor deficiencies. If I forgot to wash the dishes and the next person remembered he has not turned the lights off and the other remembers he did not bring his phone and cannot respond to his wife's inquiries and we all dropped what we were doing and ran to correct those minor problems immediately, the whole society's knowledge processing activities will collapse. No one will be producing the knowledge-packets we know as goods and services. In addition, how much "anger" would such interruptions cause?

The question is not that the minor deficiencies should not be addressed, but that one should not rush and more importantly, one should not address them at the expense of knowledge processing that supports the organized society. Thus the rush-based, drop everything way of addressing minor knowledge-giving deficiencies does not align with the operational beatitudes. Therefore, the test's third part of the multiple-choice test cannot be the correct choice. We move on to the last part of the test.

Consider the fourth part in the multiple-choice test. It says:

> 5:25 Agree with thine adversary quickly, whiles thou art in the way with him; lest at any time the adversary deliver thee to the judge, and the judge deliver thee to the officer, and thou be cast into prison.

> 5:26 Verily I say unto thee, Thou shalt by no means come out thence, till thou hast paid the uttermost farthing.

Just in case, in taking the test, we have not understood the presence of "brute force" in all the choices, in the fourth part we are given the alternative of "agreeing with the adversary," for otherwise we will be exposed to the societal brute force in the form of judge, officer, and prison and lose resources in the form of time and fines. This is a force-based view of life. It says, "stop knowledge seeking and knowledge sharing" in order to understand the knowledge-giving deficiencies that have created an adversarial situation. Instead, trust that by stopping the flow of knowledge, and accepting the brute force threats as solution, you engage in proper way of human behavior. Yet we know this is the exact opposite of the divine teaching in the beatitudes. An adversary and the associated anger signal the presence of "knowledge-giving deficiency." To lean toward brute force in order to address the knowledge-giving deficiency is the exact opposite of what we have learned from the divine knowledge. In the fourth part of the multiple-choice test we arrive at "screw the knowledge-based justice; just avoid exposure to brute force." Here one faces a situation of serious knowledge-giving deficiency in interaction with another human labeled the "adversary."

Should one transfer resources to others so that one would not face the question of fair application of force and fair allocation of resources—namely, justice? The fourth beatitude emphasizes the perpetual dedication the human must have toward balancing the application of force and allocation of resources. Each "imbalance" indicates the presence of knowledge-giving deficiencies that must be addressed. Is it "just" to make a quick agreement to shy away from those that use brute force to balance the society's force and resources? More importantly, would such resource transfer address or only hide the knowledge-giving deficiency that lurks under the adversarial relationship?

The approach offered in the fourth part of the test is "to fear the brute force." Is "fear of brute force" a solution to human interactions? Is it a technique of force management? Is it a good technique of force management? We know, to the contrary, it is the "balancing of force" that lies at the essence of justice. Any imbalance requires knowledge processing in order to bring it into balance. "Force" is an ever present aspect of life in the universe. There is no way of eliminating it. Therefore, force must be managed. In the same manner that by steering we apply the engine force to the force of traction so that the car stays on the road, "justice" is the method of managing force in human interactions so that everyone remains on the road of the extended force and not thrown off of it into the wilderness of brute force and harm.

The fourth part in the test does not meet the knowledge management requirements of the first beatitude, nor the force and resource management requirements of the fourth beatitude. This part of the multiple-choice test also cannot be correct.

The test is about human relationships, a multiple-choice test, yet we face the unexpected outcome that all choices are false, none the correct answer. What is the divine doing to us? Let us stop and think about what we have observed so far. Four choices and none strikes us as right, so what are we to do with the four choices we have been given in the test? Which one of the four wrong answers should we choose as our answer? The answer: none of them. All of them are wrong answers for the human that has chosen to follow the path of the beatitudes as way of human life. If so, as knowledge processors, we have to ask, why does the divine give a multiple-choice test in which none of the choices are correct? It is clear that the divine is not trying to run a class in the traditional sense where the right answer is placed among the wrong answers. With this design of the multiple-choice test, is the divine trying to teach us another fundamental aspect of life?

Even with earthly teachers, a test is never just to check what one has learned, it is also a teaching tool to make the student learn new things beyond what has been covered in class. So what else is the divine teaching us? Does the divine tell us that so long as we live in the force-based resource taking system, our current condition, it would NEVER offer us an alternative that does not include reliance on brute force? The test represents examples of what the current societies offer to humans, everything set up according to brute force as the foundation. The four steps in the beatitudes are the starting point for switching from the force-based foundation to the knowledge-based foundation. The test rejects all force-based alternatives when life is viewed in terms of the divine knowledge in the beatitudes.

Are there other explanations? Like any good knowledge processor let us check our knowledge processing steps. We have started with the divine knowledge in the beatitudes. We have learned that knowledge and have been tested in order to check our degree of understanding. We have given the correct answer to the test as "none of the above," but "none of the above" is implicit in the test. It has not been given explicitly. We have diligently reviewed all parts in the test and have run out of possibilities for the correct answer to reside among the multiple-choice parts. The only correct answer is "to follow the first four beatitudes" in human interactions, and that answer has not been included in the test. Is this a dilemma for understanding the purpose of the test? Or does it entail a foundational view in applying the divine knowledge in the beatitudes to human interactions beginning at the currently existing knowledge base and knowledge processing capabilities?

How is it possible that we apply the beatitudes to a multiple-choice test and none of the choices turns out to be the correct answer? In asking how that is possible we arrive at another insight that the test intends to deliver. That at present, even though armed with the divine knowledge of the beatitudes, we lack the knowledge to identify the alternative most suitable to human life. We do not know and cannot know the correct answer because we do not have the knowledge base and the knowledge processing capabilities to do so.

The first test is about how humans relate to humans. If we notice that we know little as to how humans relate to humans, we have to seek knowledge, share knowledge, and continue applying the beatitudes to our lives until we arrive at the right answer as to how humans are to relate to humans. It is at this moment that I think of a mundane example. Consider the following multiple-choice test. Tell me what you think is the right answer:

It is said: a) Eat monkey brain.

I say: b) Eat fried tarantula.

                 c) Eat balut.

                 d) Eat rendang.

I am the one taking the test. The test is clearly about what humans eat, but I lack the knowledge of ingredients and how they are prepared. More important, I lack the knowledge of whether my body would accept and accommodate the look, taste, and feel of such foods. In short, I am facing substantial knowledge-giving deficiencies in considering any of these choices. Therefore, the only choice that remains is to return to the first beatitude and start gaining knowledge through seeking and sharing. Without a larger knowledge base and higher knowledge processing skills, I would be incapable of facing and answering the multiple-choice question placed in front of me.

How different are the Sermon on the Mount tests from the food test above? The only difference is that the focus of the Sermon on the Mount tests is on critical aspects of human life, like how humans relate to humans, rather than on exotic foods. Otherwise, fundamentally they are the same and primarily point at the knowledge-giving deficiencies humans face in life.

We have developed some understanding of the first multiple-choice test on divine knowledge in the beatitudes. There are other tests, but we will not cover them here. Those will be in another book. But before leaving the tests it is useful to visit the traditional views of the tests. How does the millennia-old traditional view see the test we just took? It will be good to hear from the old-timers. The traditional view recognizes that the tests are founded on knowledge processing—the hermeneutical principles, but it is at a loss as to how to get started. It does not know what to do with the test.

Let me digress and tell you a personal story. I recall my father taking the family to a countryside picnic when I was about 7-8 years old. He liked to take the radio with him to listen to news and music. Those days the radios were large. I might be exaggerating, but it seemed like a big box one foot thick, two foot tall and three foot wide. It could operate on battery or electricity and in the countryside the battery was the only alternative. What makes me remember that specific day was the village woman walking past our picnic as a male singer was singing on the radio. She turned toward the radio and said, "What a lovely voice you have, you wonderful tiny little man in that box." We all laughed at the degree of her imagination and her lack of knowledge of the radio. But today, I am not laughing. I see the traditional view in that same exact position. It is hearing what the divine is saying in the "box" made of six tests but remains incapable of understanding the internals of the test or the purpose.

The traditional view has named the tests the "antitheses" and has declared them "most controversial" and "most intriguing" parts of the New Testament whose logic and rationale for the arrangement have eluded the human mind.[40] We are told that the name "antitheses" was given to the tests by Marcion in the second century. For him the naming was a design declaration as each test was seen made of two alternatives, two contrasting points of view; one the way of divine that must be adopted, and the other, the way of Torah that must be thrown out. To him the antitheses were just a comparative view of the "opposition" that demanded breaking away from the Torah.

Here the traditionalist runs into a dilemma. If this is a comparison and contrast of what God said and what the divine is saying, would it not be a refutation of God or the divine? The traditional view gets around this problem by claiming that what is being rejected is not what God said, but what has been *alleged* that God has said. That is cute. The word "alleged" is a weasel word. It adds "ignorance" to what God has said. With the added ignorance of "alleged," what God says achieves a higher "ignorance content" and therefore can be doubted more readily. This is a good technique of ignorance management to support one's position. Even then, however, the traditional view remains perplexed with the absence of "conclusions" or any reasoning as to the items given in the antitheses. They are simply stated, nothing else. From our perspective there is no such confusion because we know that they are multiple-choice questions that the justification and conclusion for each item does not come from the test being given but from the knowledge that has been studied for the test and the analysis done by the one taking the test.

Following the traditionalist, let us have a closer look at the first multiple-choice test, the one we have already taken. To the traditionalist this is the first antithesis. The traditional view names the first antithesis "murder" and observes that it draws no conclusions and leaves the reader to decide its meaning.[41] I have named the first test "human interactions" with the realization that it does not state any conclusions because it is a multiple-choice test. The test-taker decides among the choices. For clarity, let me show the first part of the test:

> [5:21] Ye have heard that it was said of them of old time, Thou shalt not kill; and whosoever shall kill shall be in danger of the judgment.

To the traditional view this is how the "men of old" rejected "murder" without rejecting the Torah and the divine commands about the same subject.[42] Note that the traditionalist is playing with the suitcase words "kill" and "murder." For Torah it is the word "kill" that applies, for the antitheses "murder." This is a game of hiding behind the suitcase words than understanding the first part of the test.

The traditional view then turns to the second part of the test:

> 5:22 But I say unto you, That whosoever is angry with his brother without a cause shall be in danger of the judgment: and whosoever shall say to his brother, Raca, shall be in danger of the council: but whosoever shall say, Thou fool, shall be in danger of hell fire.

The traditional view sees the obvious: the "murder" in the first part of the test is replaced with "anger" in the second part. Here the traditional view gets stuck what to do with the transition it claims to have taken place. It cannot explain how "anger" can become a criminal offense like murder. Since this does not make sense, other models get constructed to make it seem sensible. Here are two such models. The first model argues that this is a satirical statement intended to ridicule the first part of the multiple-choice test. The second model takes the position that the purpose is to introduce anger as "root cause" of murder.[43] From there the traditional view moves on to the third part of the test:

> 5:23 Therefore if thou bring thy gift to the altar, and there rememberest that thy brother hath ought against thee;

> 5:24 Leave there thy gift before the altar, and go thy way; first be reconciled to thy brother, and then come and offer thy gift.

Here the traditional view sees a case of "reconciliation" in an unclear situation as to who is at fault. Among possible activities which one is to be taken care of first, a perceived grudge against another person or a prearranged act of knowledge processing, the offering of a gift to the divine? It is not clear how the grudge reconciliation is to take place and how long it would take or whether it can even be reached at the existing level of knowledge. For the traditional view these are just illustrative parodies—deliberate comic exaggerations of the law that was given in the first part of the test. In the traditional mindset, the parody continues with another example in the next part involving a legal conflict.[44]

> 5:25 Agree with thine adversary quickly, whiles thou art in the way with him; lest at any time the adversary deliver thee to the judge, and the judge deliver thee to the officer, and thou be cast into prison.

> 5:26 Verily I say unto thee, Thou shalt by no means come out thence, till thou hast paid the uttermost farthing.

This is seen as an out of court settlement. The one taking the initiative to satisfy the claims of the adversary gives up any claims he might have. In this parody the one seeking a court-based resolution is deemed a fool that would land in jail. The traditional view persists in telling a "satirical story" while observing that no basis is given for drawing such a conclusion. So where does the traditionalist end in the first test—the first antithesis?

In the traditional view, the first multiple-choice test is a *comic imitation* on the test's first part, ridiculing the reciprocity-based view on murder. Not only does this conclusion have no connection to the beatitudes, it undermines the divine teaching as a comedy show on ways of the ancients. In doing so, the traditionalist declares the Sermon on the Mount irrelevant to individual life in human societies. But we know better. We are given the divine knowledge. We are being tested by the divine. Following the divine knowledge in the beatitudes and taking the test to prove that we have understood it, do we now understand that the divine knowledge is critical to human well-being and survival especially when facing the cosmic event on its way to the earth to create the canopied skies?

VIII

Applying What We Have Learned

The modern story of "case study" goes something like this. About one hundred years ago the Harvard Business School developed a novel approach to teaching and called it the *case study method*. It utilized true business stories to instruct students. In the classroom, students joined the professor in analyzing the details of a business situation—the case study. The case studies were stories that carried an embedded educational message, stories that could be seen and interpreted in a variety of ways. As such, they would teach case studies in a variety of ways.

Here is the traditionalist dilemma. If humans created this technique a century ago, how could the divine have known about it two thousand years ago? Impossible! I am sarcastic and laughing at the top of my lungs, but still we humans have such lowly view of the divine, often seeing the divine as a poor, ignorant Palestinian Jew when it comes to modern contrivances. So, what are we going to do with the case studies? All of the Sermon on the Mount's case studies we face will be analyzed and studied in detail in another book. Here, in this book, I intend to do two things. First is to make you familiar with the list of the Sermon on the Mount's case studies, a list prepared by traditionalists (which is fine). Second, in order to get a better feel for how the case studies relate to the divine knowledge in the beatitudes is to do one of the case studies.

The traditional view of the Sermon on the Mount sees and names four categories of case studies:

1. Cultic instruction 6:1-18
2. Conduct of daily life 6:19-7:12
3. Eschatological warnings 7:13-23
4. Parable of the two builders 7:24-27

Three of these categories are broken down into more case studies. The "cultic instruction" category consists of five case studies.[45]

1. Almsgiving 6:1-4
2. Praying 6:5-8
3. Lord's Prayer 6:9-13
4. Trespassing 6:14-15
5. Fasting 6:16-18

The "conduct of daily life" category consists of eight case studies.[46]

1. On treasure 6:19-21
2. On vision 6:22-23
3. On serving two masters 6:24
4. On anxiety 6:25-34
5. On judging 7:1-5
6. On profaning the holy 7:6
7. On giving and receiving 7:7-11
8. The golden rule 7:12

The "eschatological warnings" category consists of three case studies:[47]

1. Two ways and two gates 7:13-14
2. The false prophets 7:15-20
3. On self-delusion 7:21-23

The last case study is the "parable of the two builders," Matthew 24-27.

Thus the traditional view sees seventeen case studies. All case studies are about the *daily human life*. They cover all aspects of daily life. The divine knowledge in the beatitudes is to be applied to each case study. Note that to do the case studies you have to satisfy two prerequisites. First, you must have understood the divine knowledge in the beatitudes. Second, you must have successfully passed the six tests. All of these are determined by the individual choosing to follow the way of the Sermon on the Mount. The individual is the judge of whether one has understood the divine knowledge and passed the tests. Given the prerequisites, the case studies practice applying the divine knowledge to daily human life. Even though it is possible that some of you reading this book have not understood the first four steps in the beatitudes and have only seen me taking the first test, I am going to let you participate in this case study as a learning exercise. That is what professors do. I will be analyzing the case study and you will be observing.

So, let us start. Our first case study comes from the case the traditionalists place in the cultic instruction segment under the name "almsgiving 6:1-4." It tells the following story.

> 6:1 Take heed that ye do not your alms before men, to be seen of them: otherwise ye have no reward of your Father which is in heaven. 6:2 Therefore when thou doest thine alms, do not sound a trumpet before thee, as the hypocrites do in the synagogues and in the streets, that they may have glory of men. Verily I say unto you, They have their reward. 6:3 But when thou doest alms, let not thy left hand know what thy right hand

doeth: [6:4] That thine alms may be in secret: and thy Father which seeth in secret himself shall reward thee openly.

How can we analyze this story, this case study? What does it tell us about the human life when viewed in the light of the divine knowledge in the beatitudes? The case study's story is about alms. What is "alms?" How do we model "alms?" Historically, alms is food or money given to the poor, a handout or gift, and its key feature is the one-sided resource transfer among humans. In human societies, often, one-sided resource transfers happen to the "excluded." To better understand the situation we need to first understand the "excluded." Who are they? How do they come to exist, and more importantly, why do they need resource transfers?

Recall, humans share capabilities to produce goods and services, collectively creating the "societal pool of goods and services," the "market." Human access to the market, the societal pool of goods and services, is conditioned on "resource balance." Whatever one takes out from the market, one has to put back in an equivalent. That is how the market becomes self-sustaining and persists in serving human life.

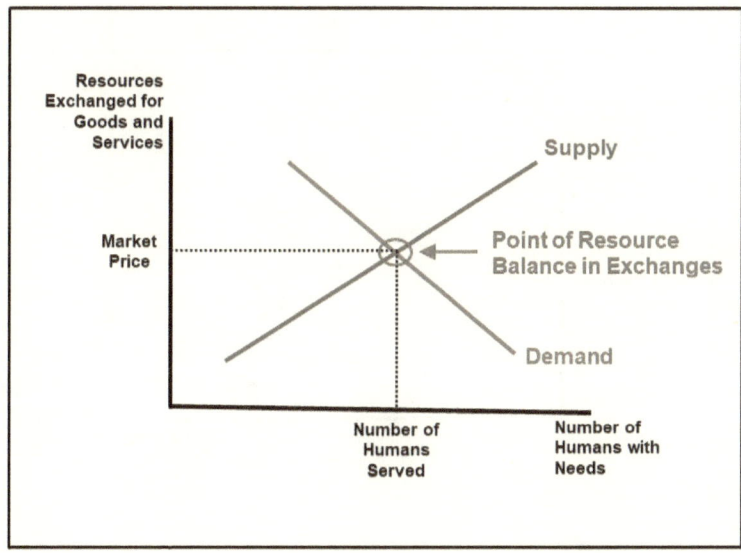

How does the market set its position of "resource balance?" Humans dealing in the market have always defined the point of balance in terms of the quantity and price of goods and services that are produced and taken out of the market, namely the societal pool of goods and services. The market's point of resource balance is called the "market equilibrium." The price and quantity at the market equilibrium reflect the condition of balance between the makers and users *willing* and *able* to engage in an exchange of goods and services.

It is in this "balancing act" that we see the "excluded" show up. They are humans that want to access the societal pool of goods and services, but cannot do so. They cannot maintain the market balance by paying the market price. They lack the resources to pay the price that maintains the market's resource balance. So here we have a dilemma. On one hand we have to maintain the market's resource balance as a market out of balance dies out and adversely affects everyone's access to goods and services. On the other hand we have humans that cannot access the market to get what they need in goods and services for daily life. They are humans, yet they are excluded from what humans do collectively, namely sharing capabilities to produce and distribute goods and services for the daily needs of all.

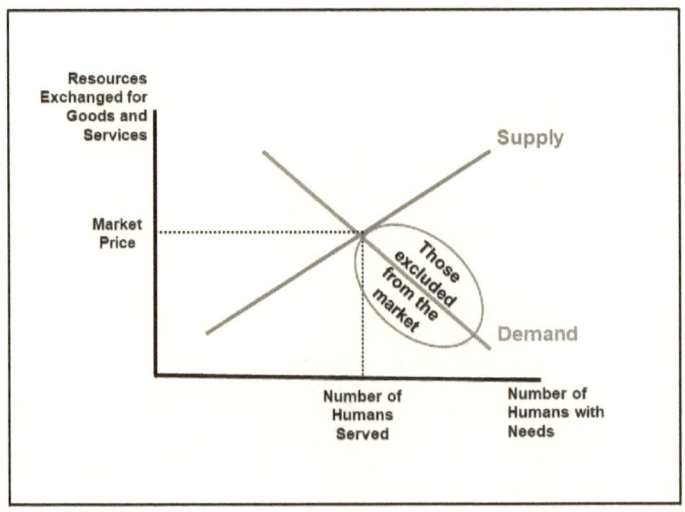

The exclusion is an inherent aspect of the market's resource balance, driven by the need for "resource balance" essential for market continuity, sustainability, and survival. Still, we cannot and should not declare the excluded as sacrificial lambs humans must offer to the market as outcome of the societal capability sharing.

The excluded are the outcome of human interactions in the exchange-based resource taking system, the outcome of how humans share capabilities. More important, the excluded are humans—force appliers, resource takers, and knowledge processors. They are willing to participate in the market, they want to share their capabilities, they want to access the societal pool of goods and services, and they need the goods and services for daily life, but are not able to do so. They lack the resources to meet the market price with "price" being a necessary measure of resource balance in human interactions.

The key question. What are we to do with the excluded? The historical answer, help them out to reach a better position of balance in relation to the market. In historical language: give the excluded alms. The alms are one-sided resource transfers to improve the excluded's chance of accessing the market and paying the market price for goods and services. The alms improve the human ability to remain in resource balance in relation to the market. The case study is about "resource transfers" to the excluded. It is about management of humans thrown out of the societal sharing system, humans that must somehow be brought back into the societal sharing system.

The case study declares alms, the act of one-sided resource transfers, as a "few-agree position." The individual that owns resources decides what amount is to be transferred, to whom it is to be transferred, and the frequency of such transfers. Everything is to be kept a secret only known to the donor and recipient. This makes "secrecy" the first key feature of the case study. Yet every form of secrecy is a "knowledge-giving deficiency" to those not involved in the secret. Secrecy propagates the knowledge-giving deficiency; at minimum, the knowledge of who is excluded, how the exclusion has come about, and how it can be addressed. It keeps the excluded outside of the capability sharing possibilities of all those not part of the secret. The secrecy goes against the first beatitude that highlights identifying and addressing knowledge-giving deficiencies and remedying them through knowledge seeking and knowledge sharing.

Everything humans make and use are knowledge-packets. All goods and services are knowledge-packets, outcomes of societal knowledge seeking and knowledge sharing. When someone cannot get the goods and services needed for daily life, that individual lacks the needed knowledge-packets. Lacking the needed knowledge-packets is a serious "knowledge-giving deficiency." Secrecy is a device of hiding knowledge-giving deficiencies. Anything "secret" is a knowledge deficiency because it is not shared societally. The more a society becomes secretive, the greater its knowledge-giving deficiencies.

The first beatitude teaches us that when dealing with the excluded we cannot keep it secret. Consider the inadequate resource position of the alms recipient. The resource imbalance is the outcome of individual and societal knowledge-giving deficiencies. It must be addressed through knowledge seeking and knowledge sharing and not through secretive acts. The problem of the excluded and the resource transfers that address the exclusion is not a few-agree concern among secretive individuals but a societal, many-agree concern that must be addressed through knowledge seeking and knowledge sharing at the societal level. In the case study, every admonition about not telling anyone about the "resource transfers" falls into the category of "not sharing knowledge" with others. According to the first beatitude, it undermines every human's life as it drags the society into deeper knowledge-giving deficiencies.

The case study also warns of a trap, the suitcase word trap. In the case study the trap is formed by the suitcase word "Father." It is easy to use a suitcase word as means of support and justification. Humans do it all the time. It is ignorance management and the suitcase word "Father" is the source of ignorance being added to the situation. The case study points at the suitcase word Father and claims it will balance out the secretive, few-agree individual behavior in resource transfers. That is a false claim. Adding a suitcase word to the mix of secrets only increases the level of ignorance, the level of knowledge-giving deficiencies about the excluded and their resource position. It would exacerbate the mourning situations, not bringing them into everyone's full view through knowledge seeking and knowledge sharing.

In a knowledge-based society, nothing *secretive* would be adopted as the norm for managing societal resource transfers. The traditional view claims that secrecy in resource transfers is needed in order to protect the "eschatological reward" that the Father will provide.[48] In other words we will benefit in the canopied earth if we are good in hiding the resource transfers to the excluded others. We know such argument is false as any hidden resource transfer is a "societally deficient flow of knowledge." Such deficiency becomes the worst when facing the eschaton—the transition from one earth version to the other.

Consider the logic that the case study offers in support of secretive, individual-based resource transfers. It asserts that keeping the resource transfers secretive is better than using the resource transfers to "show off." It compares two bad behaviors, chooses the one less troubling. The "showing off" accomplishes little knowledge processing in relation to the knowledge-giving deficiencies that cause the exclusion. At best, "showing off" is the behavior of a successful resource taker that has no understanding of the societal sharing system. The individual seeks to convert the "showing off" into more resources. The show-off individual that uses one-sided resource transfers as a device of extracting more resources from others is as bad as the one that makes the transfer of resources a personal, secretive, few-agree position. Neither human recognizes the "knowledge-giving deficiency" in their own behavior. They are not walking the way of the beatitudes. Both the logic of secretive self-control of resource transfers and showing off in the hope of developing an improved position of privilege that will yield greater resource taking opportunities are behaviors normal to the force-based system as it exists today. They are not behaviors of those following the knowledge-based path of the beatitudes.

Let me now change our perspective. We are no longer interested in the situation of almsgiving totally hidden from the public view. Instead we are interested in knowing what the society does when the almsgiving is in plain sight. Consider a visible system of one-sided resource transfers based on individual few-agree positions. It happens in a very large city, New Delhi, India. There, 500,000 children work in the streets tapping on car windows as beggars asking for handouts. Some also sell magazines and boxes of facial tissue to potential buyers, thus a system of almsgiving either through begging or selling something. The beggar, the mechanism of almsgiving.

In the New Delhi system of almsgiving nothing is secretive. It is exposed to societal observers; the transactions are not confined to the giver and receiver of alms. What does a force-based system do in this situation? In New Delhi, politicians, the society's force managers, have set up force extensions to fine the drivers if they give anything to the beggars. The purpose is not to address the knowledge-giving deficiencies that create the begging, but to speed up the flow of traffic and to change the image of the city and country as a locus of beggars. Brute force deemed as solution. What does brute force in guise of force extensions achieve? It forces many drivers not to give alms or buy things from the street children. Some children see this as job loss and return to their villages, others see it as signal to move away from car traffic to other begging locations such as temples and mosques. In all this the "knowledge-giving deficiency" that creates the excluded, in this case the children, is left untouched. If this is how knowledge-giving deficiencies are addressed when almsgiving is directly visible, how would the knowledge-giving deficiencies be addressed if the almsgiving remains invisible?

So where are we? In this case study we come face-to-face with the biggest problem in human societies, the situation of the excluded. Almost all societies eventually collapse when they cannot manage the situation of the excluded. The pain of intense knowledge-giving deficiencies turns into a firestorm of brute force in the form of revolts and revolutions released on everyone, destroying everything. The society collapses. One of the biggest challenges that humans face in the first two steps of the beatitudes is to recognize and manage the combination of knowledge-giving deficiency and mourning situation called "the excluded."

¤ ¤ ¤

We have completed part of our journey. We started at divine knowledge, the operational beatitudes, the first four steps. We took a test on whether we have understood the divine knowledge. Then we applied what we know to a case study, a real-life situation. We are now ready to take more tests and do more case studies. After that we will be ready to start the transformation that sets the world's societal sharing system to walk through the swarm and be as functional and human-serving in the canopied earth as it was in the blue-skied earth. Amen!

IX

Another Look at What We Learned so Far

The first four beatitudes, the operational aspects of human life, start with knowledge-giving deficiencies, move into addressing mourning situations, then gentle assessing of alternatives, and ends in a justice system that balances the human differences and differentials. I have already said the operational side of the beatitudes comes first, then the beatitudes' perfection side. The second set of four beatitudes points the way toward "perfection" of the operational aspects set up in the first four beatitudes.

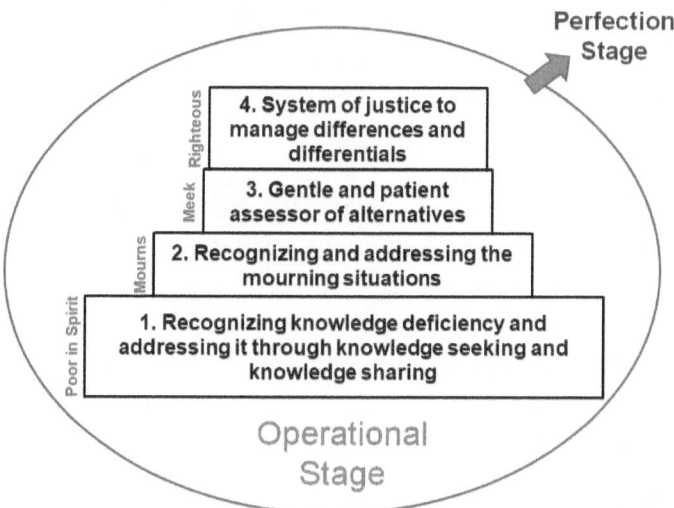

In my point of view of human societies, there is no way to consider "perfection." No way! In taking care of the world and the human societies we can at best hope to handle the first four beatitudes. For the knowledge-deficient human, adopting the knowledge-based path of life in the Sermon on the Mount is a question of human capabilities. Given our current capabilities we will spend a long time adopting and improving our alignment with each of the first four steps. We can endeavor to excel in knowledge giving—the seeking and sharing of knowledge. We can constantly improve our ability to mourn, our ability to identify and address the mourning situations. We can work on patient and gentle assessment of alternatives from which we will chose the ways of producing and distributing goods and services for all. This is especially demanding when managing the society's mix of many-agree positions at assemblies we know as the House of Representatives and the Senate. And finally, we will set up and manage a system of application of force and allocation of resources in balance with all the differences and differentials that human uniqueness brings to life. Over a long time such acts would improve the societal sharing system in serving the needs of all in daily life, especially the excluded. But at this time we lack the capabilities to deliver us into perfection. Becoming good in the first four beatitudes creates a base from which we can take off toward perfection, but at this time the second set of four beatitudes, the way toward perfection, can wait.

We have started with the basic assumption that the Sermon on the Mount is divine knowledge. If so, what have we learned from seeing, coming face to face with a piece of divine knowledge? Even if we never use any of it in life, we should be able to say what we have seen. It is like seeing a car and never choosing to drive it. We should be able to say what was saw in the car. Here is my take. In the Sermon on the Mount certain attributes of "divine knowledge" stand out:

1. Divine knowledge is "compact," like the beatitudes.
2. Divine knowledge is "universal," applicable to all with no religious prerequisites, with no "religion business" design to the divine knowledge.
3. Divine knowledge is not a force-based structure. Anytime "force" is highlighted, it signals we're dealing with human-developed knowledge, not divine knowledge.
4. Divine knowledge is not given as "absolute." It always gives the human choice. To follow or not is always conditional on human choice.

In my mind, these observations are the rules of thumb for assessing whether a piece of knowledge in the sacred texts comes from a divine source or from humans that put together the sacred texts. Given these criteria, in all sacred texts I have read, I have not come across anything resembling the Sermon on the Mount. I have seen no other piece of knowledge that comes with the attributes of compactness, universality, absence of force, and conditionality. If you see one, please let me know.

What else have we learned from looking at the Sermon on the Mount? We have learned about the "human nature." It implies certain things about the human nature. The human is:

1. Knowledge seeker, knowledge sharer.
2. Other-feeler, especially in bad situations, the mourning situations.
3. Gentle and patient force applier. Alternative seeker so that brute force is not applied on humans.
4. Justice seeker, manager of differences and differentials in a fair way with "fair" dependent on knowledge seeking and knowledge sharing capabilities.

When reading the Sermon on the Mount one might come to the conclusion that the divine does not want to make "divine knowledge" easy. Why doesn't the divine just tell us the rules of life and the consequences of not obeying? Life would be so much easier. That is the typical expectation, but its first big problem is that it is a "force-first system." It is founded on brute force that the human expects the divine would exert on humans. If the divine wants to teach us a knowledge-based system the divine would not start at brute force. If the divine wanted us to be stuck in a force-based, command-driven structure, then there would be no tests and no case studies. But they exist. There is no command structure in the Sermon on the Mount, only a knowledge-based view of life.

How many words would a divine being need in order to provide information to humans? Can the divine being say what the divine means using a handful of words? Or, does the divine have to write thick tombs in order to express the divine knowledge fully? I take the position that, despite all deficiencies and ignorance content in human-made words, a divine being should be able to state every foundational view of life in a few words. This has been the case even when the divine has used the ignorance-filled, human-made words that humans use for communication. Otherwise the divine being would not be divine and merely resemble another human. So, look at the Sermon on the Mount and see the divine presence. The eight lines in the beatitudes is all the divine needs. Only half of that to set up the human life, the other half to lead the human life toward perfection. What about the rest of the Sermon on the Mount? Only tests and case studies set up to suite the human capabilities so humans would learn to apply the knowledge of the beatitudes to specific situations of life in order to develop a deeper understanding.

One other thing we hopefully have learned and will never forget. Anytime we encounter something in the Sermon on the Mount that seems wrong or confusing, it should signal our own knowledge deficiency rather than bad divine knowledge. This does not mean that those who received the divine knowledge did not add, delete, or alter it to "make it right." Such behavior is most embedded in ignorant humans, changing the knowledge to match the human ignorance. With the beatitudes, however, we can almost be certain that it is unaltered divine knowledge. At the same time, "not understanding" always confuses the human. The "tests" are where the confusion peaks. The test is like answering to the divine—extremely difficult for the unprepared.

¤ ¤ ¤

What else have we learned? How do we see those that claim the Sermon on the Mount has nothing to do with the masses? Those that declare the Sermon on the Mount as an ideal that only few humans might be able to reach? Those that do not recognize the prime impediment to achieving the way of the Sermon on the Mount comes from the human inability to manage brute force? With our current knowledge base and knowledge processing capabilities, we cannot manage "harm throwing" which is the main feature of brute force. Brute force when applied on human always acts as "harm thrower." Every gun is a "harm thrower." Every army is a "harm thrower." And ironically, humans, though totally incapable of managing "harm throwers," constantly seek to build and use bigger "harm throwers." The Sermon on the Mount takes its ultimate shape within the context of *no brute force* applied on humans, no acts of "harm throwing" directed at humans. From this perspective, its full implementation becomes conditional on humans excelling in brute force management.

What else have we learned? Not to dismiss the persistent

rejection of the Sermon on the Mount as something bad. What? It is possible that the rejection reflects human wisdom and that human wisdom is better for humans than divine wisdom. How is that possible? The Sermon on the Mount is a knowledge-based societal sharing system. Throughout history, the societal sharing system consistently chosen by humans for their societies has been force-based. It reflects the existing level of human capabilities. Is it possible that humans have come to the correct conclusion that the force-based social structure is the only arrangement they can manage? That the knowledge-based way of the Sermon on the Mount is way out of their league?

If the divine tells me that basketball and dunking the ball is the best way to stay physically healthy and I cannot even dribble the ball let alone dunk, it is inevitable that I would wisely choose "walking" as way of exercising over basketball. I am good in walking and can manage it well, but I am not good in basketball and can only manage it poorly. What God has given is definitely great, but what could I do with it in my life when I cannot use it? What I am capable of doing can be quite different from what God wants me to do. This type of comparative assessment has happened for millennia. Over millennia the societal leaders, especially the CEOs of religion business, have concluded that humans are only capable of organizing themselves according to a force-based system, even though it constantly exposes everyone to the danger of concentrated brute force. They all hope that eventually humans can get better in managing the "harm throwers" that litter their lives. In their view the knowledge-based system would collapse because of the human inability to manage it.

Since there is no backup to the knowledge-based system but the force-based system, why choose the knowledge-based system where humans lack management skill? This we need to keep in mind, a deep question of the level of human capabilities. The existing levels of human capability might require staying a lot longer with the force-based system while keeping the knowledge-based system and its required capabilities in the back of our mind as something humans must strive to develop.

There is a problem with gradually switching from the force-based system to a knowledge-based system. This really big problem is the management of swarm crossing when the earth becomes canopied. The transition between the earth's two versions can be best achieved in the knowledge-based mode. Staying with the force-based system can be a recipe for human annihilation. What should we do? This is like saying I am not good at playing basketball, but have to play it. My survival and well-being depends on it. Can I play well when I really have to play?

Perhaps that is it. In our individual and societal choice making we have never brought in the canopied earth. Being prepared for the canopied earth is quite different from what we have done year after year under the blue skies. In all this, it is important to note the inherent simplicity of the force-based system. The boss and worker know the basis of their relationship. The boss is higher up in force hierarchy, therefore, can hire (give life to capability sharer) or fire (throw the capability sharer into economic death). It is such a simple and well-understood arrangement. The one with the lower force position always seeks to perform and please the one with the higher force position. The one at the higher position is protected by the societal concentrated force and exerts control on those in lower force positions. But such is not the case when we switch from force-based to knowledge-based. The worker would not "fake working" and now would share that what he does is irrelevant to organization's needs and that it is better to move out and apply capabilities elsewhere. The boss will now share that he doesn't know how to manage the organization well and one from among the workers or from outside has to take care of managing the organization. Can you imagine that? No such knowledge flow ever takes place in the force-based system. When in force-defined and force-backed positions, all parties hide their weaknesses. Any information that adversely affects their force position is never revealed. Exactly the reverse happens in the knowledge-based system. There is no hiding of knowledge in the knowledge-based system where all knowledge is shared. The force-based or knowledge-based way of life? The challenge remains. The divine suggests, the human chooses.

X

One More Time

One more time let us see the Sermon on the Mount through the lens of the business world. Assume the extreme, assume the business world knows the beatitudes. How would they implement it? Here is a picture of possibilities. In the first beatitude we are told to "focus on things we do not know or know poorly." We know that the business world does that. It is focused on addressing and removing its knowledge deficiencies. But the business world also does something else. It focuses on "what it knows" and then seeks to improve on what it knows. The business world does this regularly, focusing on what it knows and improving it in small steps. In fact, it has given it the catchy Japanese name "kaizen," or its English translation "continuous improvement."

What is the difference? Why does the divine want us to focus on our deficiencies instead of what we have already accomplished? Does the focus on "what we know" reduce our attention to converting ignorance to knowledge? Does it make the human complacent in adding small increments to what one already knows and in the process ignore the knowledge-giving deficiencies that adversely affect life? We need to seriously think about how we currently do things and how we are told to change our way. How can we not focus on what we know but focus on what we do not know?

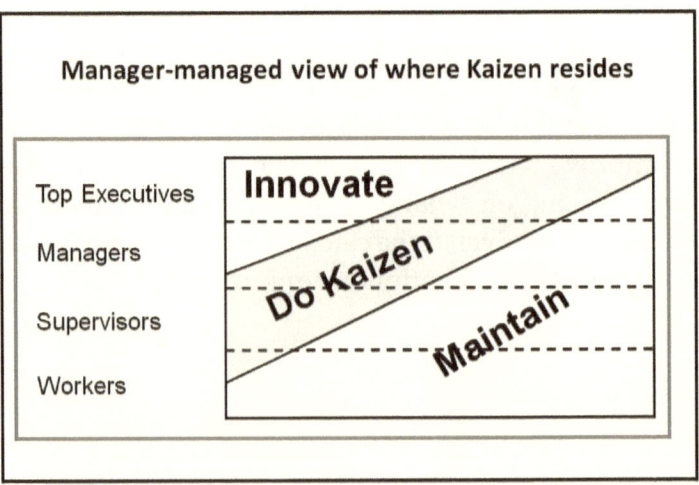

When it comes to Kaizen, the business world sees the improvement originating and happening within a certain domain. The improvement domain does not include the masses of workers, they do little "improvement." They are primarily focused on maintenance of the knowledge we already have. Even among the managers only part of their time is spent on improving the current knowledge base. The task of any major improvement, highlighted as "innovation," is left to top management. In this picture, the masses of workers are left out of contributing to major improvements in the knowledge base. That, in itself, is a major knowledge-giving deficiency. From the point of view of the masses of workers, the improvement comes primarily from the knowledge that the management throws at them without their participation in creating it. Is this one reason the beatitudes want *everyone* focused on knowledge-giving deficiencies, on what they do not know or know poorly?

The second beatitude amplifies the first by bringing extra focus on things that we do not know or know poorly and the best evidence for that is the "high levels of pain and suffering" displayed as mourning situations. Anything that produces high levels of pain and suffering points at what we do not know or know poorly. Similar to the first beatitude where the business world expresses gradual knowledge improvements under the name kaizen, in the second beatitude the business world sees certain mourning situations as "theory of constraints." What does the theory of constraints seek to address? Consider a simplistic situation. A road on which automobiles are to travel is crowded with sheep. The sheep pose a constraint to transportation. They cause a situation of pain and suffering for the drivers. What is one to do?

The theory of constraints says that the focus must be on the constraint and its removal. If instead of focusing on the sheep we focus on improving the reception of electronic devices so that the car can play better music or calling someone that studies changing the road from two lanes to four lanes. We lack focus on the pain and suffering currently at hand. The theory of constraints takes the position that before you engage in any other consideration, you must first address the bottleneck that is causing the pain and suffering. Anything else would be a waste of resources and knowledge processing capabilities.

The theory of constraints involves a five-step process: identify, exploit, subordinate, elevate, and repeat. It is a one-step-at-a-time recipe for handling the mourning situations. The first step, identify, asks if you can see the constraint, the area where the pain and suffering is visible. In business terms, the area that limits production and creates pain and suffering in the form of reduced cash flow and profitability because of reduced goods and services produced and delivered to customers. Once the constraint is identified, the second step, exploit, focuses on ways of improving the constraint using the knowledge and resources that are available at the constraint itself. In our simplistic example of the cars and the sheep, this means the driver getting out of the car to try ways of moving the sheep off the road.

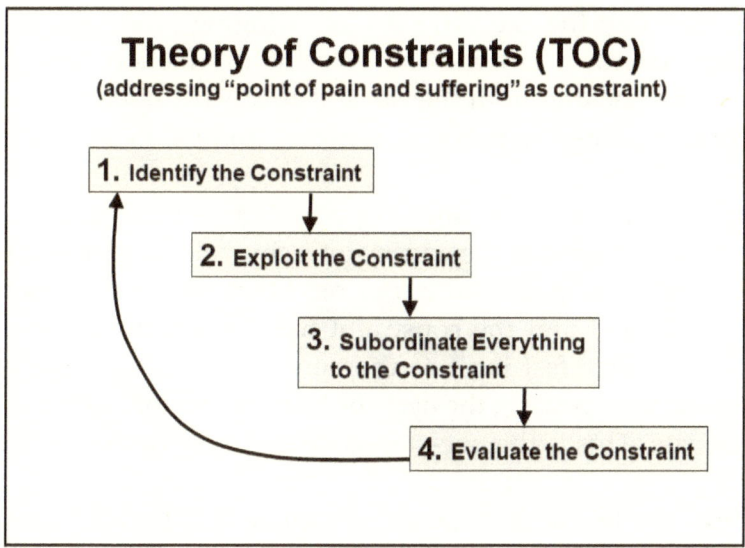

Having exhausted the possibilities for addressing the constraint with knowledge and resources available at the constraint itself, the third step, subordinate, seeks ways of using knowledge processing and knowledge base in other areas and adjusting the resources in other areas in order to take care of the constraint. This would be like transferring manpower and resources from other departments to the department that faces the constraint. The resource needs of other departments are subordinated to the needs of the department that faces the constraint, the mourning situation. In the simplistic car and sheep example, this would be like going to another car's driver, telling him to stop what he is doing and join the first driver to clear his part of the road first. Or, going outside of the car to the trees around the road, cutting branches and then trying to move the sheep by waving the branches at them. The other driver and the tree branches are the resources of other areas made available to the constraint.

If the constraint still remains a constraint, in the fourth step, elevate, the call goes out into the larger region or the higher-level managers for knowledge and resources that can help. In the business world this would be the consideration of capital investments by the executive group, bringing more wealth into the department in order to improve the production capacity to remove the constraint. In the car and sheep example, this would be like contacting the police department and the local farmers to come and help.

The theory of constraints' presumption is that the first four steps will take care of the constraint, remove it, and stop it from being a point of pain and suffering. Once the four steps have been completed and the constraint has been removed, another area would manifest itself as the new constraint and has to be addressed by repeating the cycle of identify, exploit, subordinate, and elevate. This is the one-step-at-a-time view of the mourning situations, take care of one and then start looking for the next. Is this how the beatitudes intend humans to act? I don't know. All the second beatitude is asking is whether the human is "capable of seeing" the mourning situations. The presumption is that upon seeing, humans would do something to address and remove them. After all, it is "pain and suffering."

The theory of constraint sees the constraint itself as the weakest link in how the human capabilities are shared. At the societal level, unless it is taken care of, the constraint will make the rest of the society suboptimal. Nothing would work as well as it should when the mourning situations remain. The theory of constraints also recognizes the possibility of resource conflicts when addressing a constraint and that the conflict must be resolved if the constraint is to be removed effectively. The point of resource conflict could be layers removed from the constraint under consideration and make seeing the conflict difficult without full understanding of the societal sharing system that addresses the constraint as a mourning situation. The second beatitude thus points at the higher level societal attention that must be paid to constraints and their removal and that the existing resource conflicts must also be addressed societally when removing the constraints as mourning situations.

What else does the theory of constraints teach us relevant to the second beatitude? Those that believe they are not causing the constraint would be reluctant to give up their resources in order to improve the factors that create the constraint. They are often concerned that the resources given to others might make their own resource position vulnerable to becoming a mourning situation. The society's top managers, namely the CEOs and government executives, are often reluctant to deliver wealth into the constraint that does not perform well with its own existing resources. The mourning situation signals that it is not a wealth-generator but a wealth-consumer that might turn out to be a wealth destroyer, never recovering what has been put into it to stop the mourning situation. The top managers are often concerned with pouring wealth into an area that by itself is not capable to "identify and exploit" to remove the constraint. Finally, the second beatitude's implied notion of "open flow of resources" toward the mourning situation is neither currently understood nor practiced in the business world. The business world's workplaces exist and operate mostly as localized fiefdoms with little interest in allocating their resources toward addressing the mourning situations of others.

Arriving at the third and then the fourth beatitude

From the first beatitude's focus on what we do not know and second beatitude's mindset of identifying and addressing the mourning situations, we arrive at the third beatitude. This is where we find the business world most comfortable with what the third beatitude says. Much of everything that the business world does is based on patient and gentle assessment of alternatives. It takes time to engage in knowledge processing to determine which alternative best fits the needs of others and is best sustained through wealth making. This is all done gently, avoiding the use of brute force on humans. Rarely a business tries to force an alternative on others.

This is where the business world is most aligned with the divine knowledge in the Sermon on the Mount. This is where the resource management remains focused on what humans need in their daily lives. Where this alignment breaks down is in production of weapons as "harm throwers." From the harm-thrower perspective, the business world would be the eventual destroyer of humankind with weapons of mass destruction it regularly produces for those whose sole purpose is to massively harm humans.

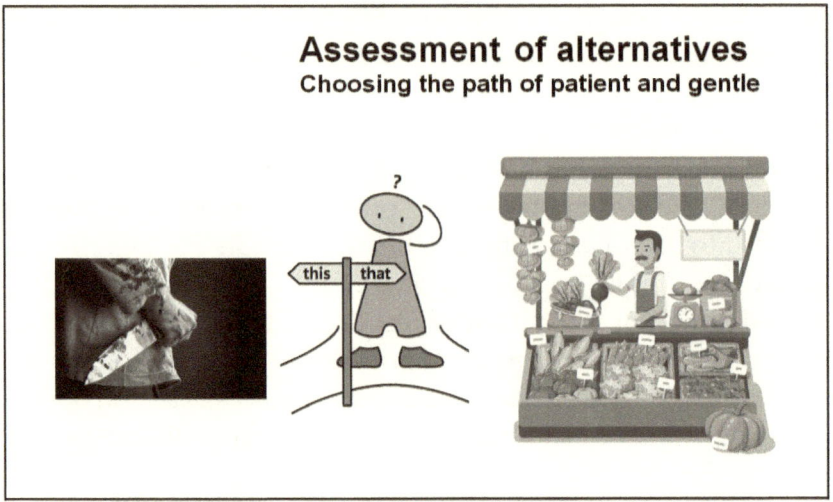

Assessment of alternatives
Choosing the path of patient and gentle

the third beatitude's gentle and patient resource management we arrive at balanced management of the force-based resource taking system. The gentle and patient management of resources happens within the society's force network. Within the force network the focus is on the market's exchange-based resource taking. The market's key requirement is that it must remain in balance, that human interactions never degrade to become brute force confrontations. This means balance in relation to goods and services that everyone needs in daily life. The balanced production and use of goods and services define "justice."

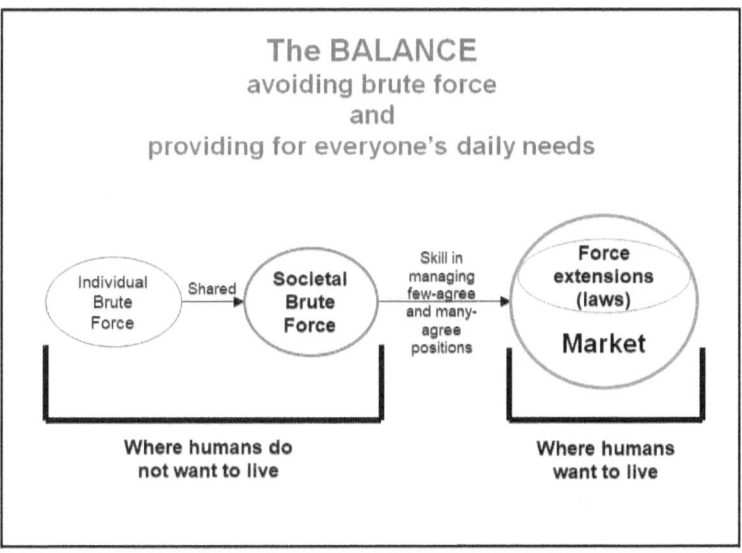

What the fourth beatitude highlights is the necessity of continually watching out for maintaining the societal balance. The fourth beatitude does not say how that balance is to be maintained and does not say how the balance should be defined. All that is left to the human as force applier, knowledge processor, and choice maker. The only thing the fourth beatitude emphasizes is that everyone, at all times and anywhere in the societal sharing system, must watch out for the balance, behave, act, and process knowledge in ways that maintain the force and resource balance. The managers of the society's many-agree positions, namely the members of the House of Representatives and the Senate, play the key role in managing the many-agree positions such that the societal force network and the market maintain their long-term balance. Any imbalance among the managers of the society's many-agree positions signals a society out of balance. While the business world seeks to maintain balance in whatever it does, its pursuit of advantageous designs of the societal force network is a regular contributor to societal imbalance.

XI

The Kingdom of Heaven as Canopied Earth

We are told that when following the way of the Sermon on the Mount we manage the "kingdom of heaven" well. But besides mentioning it, the Sermon on the Mount says nothing about the details of the "kingdom of heaven." Why? After you read my canopied earth books, you will know the answer. All sacred texts of humankind are repositories of the knowledge of the kingdom of heaven, namely the canopied earth. Most of the bible symbolism is about the canopied earth—the kingdom of heaven. No need to repeat the same in the Sermon on the Mount. How did I get to see the "kingdom of heaven" as "canopied earth"? Through divine whispers. I don't think, by myself, on my own knowledge processing, I would have ever been able to recognize the kingdom of heaven as the canopied earth.

It sounds odd that divine whispers can be used in analyzing the sacred texts and identifying the canopied earth as a foundational aspect of human existence, but it is true. Why me? I have no idea. Nonetheless, your understanding of life through this book originates at mixing the human knowledge—my decades of research and hard work—with the smallest sliver of divine knowledge received through whispers. The divine whispers are my explanation of cause and origin of unusual insights. It is a few-agree position. In the final count the divine whispers do not count. What counts is the many-agree knowledge embedded in my books. The society is built on many-agree and not on few-agree positions.

Back to other views. How does the traditional view understand the "kingdom of heaven"? We would not be surprised that the traditional understanding highlights what is good for the religion business. It is not that the religion business does not understand the "significance" of the kingdom of heaven, it does. The "kingdom of heaven" and its equivalent the "kingdom of God" are prominent in the synoptic Gospels. Even to the traditionalists of the religion business they represent a key aspect of the divine teaching, but that is where the understanding of the religion business ends because it has no understanding of the canopied earth.

The traditional meanings attached to the kingdom of heaven serve the religion business. For example, the kingdom of heaven is claimed to represent the *hearts and minds of the believers* that pursue the religion business teachings. In other words, the kingdom of heaven is the "customers of the religion business." Or in pursuit of a higher meaning, the religion business becomes bold enough to declare itself—the Church—as kingdom of heaven. While the mainstream religion business continues to see itself as kingdom of heaven, the idea of the kingdom of heaven as "radical change" remains alive. It sees the kingdom of heaven in apocalyptic terms, something to take shape in the future and cause radical change. In this view, the prominent outcome of kingdom of heaven is "eschatological" with the word eschatological coming from "eschatology" defined as pointing to the "end things." To understand the canopied earth we need to understand the language of eschatology.

Let me give you a few simple, rudimentary examples of the

eschatological view applied to daily human life. For example, the eschatological view of "day" is that it ends in "night." Or the eschatological view of "winter" would end in "spring." The eschatological view of the kingdom of heaven is traditionally seen as "end of the earth," complete transformation of earth and heavens into a radically different shape. Since this transformation is not understood, it is simply taken as "the end." Thus the eschatological viewpoints at the "end of the world." It points at "end time." The end of the world and end time are suitcase words. They are interesting, ignorance-based terminologies in that the traditional view throws them at us without saying what they mean physically.

How does the world, as we know it, end? Is there a new start? A new world? If yes, what does it look like? Further questions arise such as how "time" as we know it stops and how the new time that replaces it functions. The traditional view is incapable of giving a physical view of how the kingdom of heavens' eschatology comes about, but I can. You have seen me hinting at a preliminary view of the cosmic event in which a swarm of comet fragments alters the earth from its current form into a "canopied" form. The new earth gets surrounded by a shell of cometary material. The earth as we know it would end. It will be replaced with the canopied earth. "Time" as we know it will cease to exist as the sun would no longer rise in the east but rise in the west and set in the east. You will read about the canopied earth's details in my other books.

The "eschaton" is the "event" that produces the transition from the blue-skied to canopied earth. The Sermon on the Mount clearly teaches that those that follow its way of life become more capable of managing the eschaton confrontation, a roughly one-day celestial event in which the earth passes through a swarm of cometary fragments. The swarm crossing (the eschaton) is the end point of the blue-skied earth as we know it and the start of the canopied world. The blue-skied and canopied earths alternate, the cycle repeating every 100,000 years.

The key in all this is not to miss the fact that humans, in the past, have seen and experienced the eschaton. They have maintained millennia-old oral tradition about it. They have written about it and described it. They have written about the human condition facing the eschaton and the canopied earth it creates. Such writing fills every society's sacred texts. Today there are many more humans on earth than there were tens of thousands of years ago. As such, preparation to meet the eschaton and to live under the canopied skies is going to be more complex and challenging. I am certain that is why we are given the divine knowledge in the Sermon on the Mount so that humankind would be well prepared when facing this cosmic challenge.

The Sermon on the Mount tells us that in facing the cometary swarm's eschaton we have the choice of following the divine teaching. In that case we will end up happy and successfully deal with the canopied earth. Or we can choose to go at it in our own current, force-based way, which, by comparison, we will not be as happy. We will not be as effective in dealing with the canopied earth. The choice is with the human. The divine only the provider of knowledge.

The kingdom of heaven's double meaning

The primary focus of the "kingdom of heaven" is the eschaton, the transition between the two versions of the earth. But we don't have to limit its meaning to a physical earthly phenomenon. We can also see it in terms of the "societal sharing system" that humans create and maintain. When the societal sharing system becomes aligned with the Sermon on the Mount, it is also a form of "kingdom of heaven," a global society of the divine-aligned humans on earth. I believe we should consider both meanings when using the Sermon on the Mount as way of human life.

I am even open to the traditional idea that at present the kingdom of heaven exists in part, even though its full-scale appearance will come in a future moment referred to as the "eschaton." Why do I think that, in part, the kingdom of heaven already exists? Recall what I said about the business world's current degree of alignment with the four operational beatitudes. The business world is already acting in part according to the Sermon on the Mount. As such I can argue that, in part, the kingdom of heaven already exists on earth even though humans are not fully aware of it. Everyone on earth, and I mean everyone, is in part living according to the Sermon on the Mount and therefore is partly in the kingdom of heaven. The divine knowledge is everywhere. It is at the foundation of every aspect of human life, every aspect of the universe. It does not need to be put in a book so that it will become present. The only difference, the book form amplifies the human awareness of its existence.

Similarly, the "canopied earth," in part, is already existing on earth in two prominent forms, the scientific records and the sacred texts. The scientific records capture the remnants of the past canopied earths. The sacred texts capture the eyewitness accounts of those that experienced it thousands of years ago. The sacred tests attest to the utter significance of the canopied earth experience when declaring those observations "sacred," meaning most important for all future generations.

Right now the kingdom of heaven primarily exists as ancient human experience of the canopied earth and modern human alignment with a beatitudes-based societal sharing system. At the moment it is only in part, not in entirety. It will become complete at the eschaton. I have already said the relevance of the Sermon on the Mount to human life becomes most evident when facing the eschaton. The Sermon on the Mount is always of value to human life as the recipe for construction and maintenance of a robust societal sharing system, with or without the eschaton, in any version of the earth. But how well humans use the Sermon on the Mount depends on humans. The level of preparedness to meet the eschaton is a human choice. Ideally, when facing the eschaton, the human societies must have implemented the Sermon on the Mount a long time ago. From human experience of building and maintaining "societal sharing systems" we know it cannot be done overnight. Examples abound. It took centuries to build and maintain the societal sharing system we know as the United States of America. If an African or Middle Eastern society chooses to build its societal sharing system in the style of the United States, it will take that society centuries of capability development and capability sharing to get it done. It cannot be done when the news channels inform a cometary swarm is on its way and the earth will have a cometary canopy within the next six months.

The societal sharing system is the largest and most complex "knowledge-packet" humans put together in order to share their capabilities to provide goods and services for the daily needs of all. It cannot be redesigned and restructured in days and months. It takes at least centuries if not millennia to align the whole earth's societal sharing systems with the Sermon on the Mount. Creating the kingdom of heaven in human societies will take a very long time, not so for the celestial kingdom of heaven, the canopied earth. It gets built in one day, in a single passage through a swarm of cometary fragments. As for the societal sharing system, the earthly kingdom of heaven has to match the celestial kingdom of heaven.

Another brief look at the canopied earth

For details of cometary swarm's eschaton and canopied earth please read my other books. Here I am going to provide a brief tour within the context of knowledge-giving deficiencies, especially the intense deficiencies we know as mourning situations.

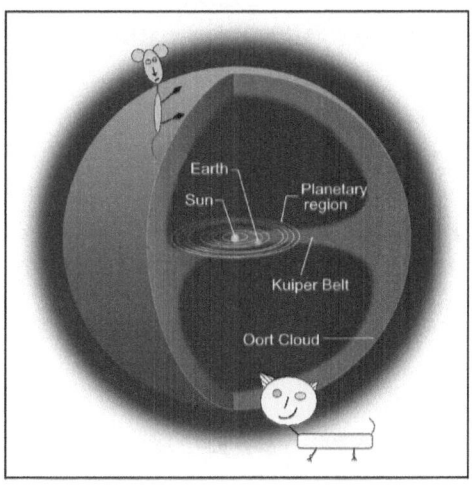

A comet is a huge ball of ice and dirt and can easily be the cause of serious mourning if it accidentally hits the earth. It requires substantial knowledge to understand what it is and what it does. So the first question we need to ask is: where does the earth, or more generally the solar system, get its comets from? What is the origin of these celestial snowballs? Not surprisingly, the comets originate at two celestial storehouses with the names Kuiper Belt and Oort Cloud. The Kuiper Belt, a disk-shaped structure, and the Oort Cloud, larger and spherical, both surround the solar system in which the earth resides. Have a look at a simple picture of these two areas from which, on occasion, comets are released earthward and occasionally get captured in orbit around the sun.

Before telling you more about these celestial storehouses let me introduce two cartoon friends, Mousy and Katzi. They will be telling us a lot more in books I have written for younger humans. Here they will help me with understanding the situation we face in eschaton. If you are wondering why I am writing books for younger humans, it is in the spirit of the first beatitude. The divine does not make the awareness of the knowledge-giving deficiencies a matter of adult humans. It is for all humans. Thus some of my books are for younger humans while most are written for adults.

With the Oort Cloud being so large, its comets, the celestial snowballs, can be affected by gravity of hundreds of millions of other suns in the Milky Way galaxy. I cannot tell you anything specific, except that the 100,000-year pattern of earthward release of comets implies something is nudging the Oort Cloud or the Kuiper Belt, kicking out a number of comets in the direction of the solar system. It is also possible that the galaxy is not the culprit. In the solar system the sun, planets, and the snowballs in the two celestial storehouses are all in dynamic motion and at some point their collective motion can also establish a pattern for releasing snowballs earthward.

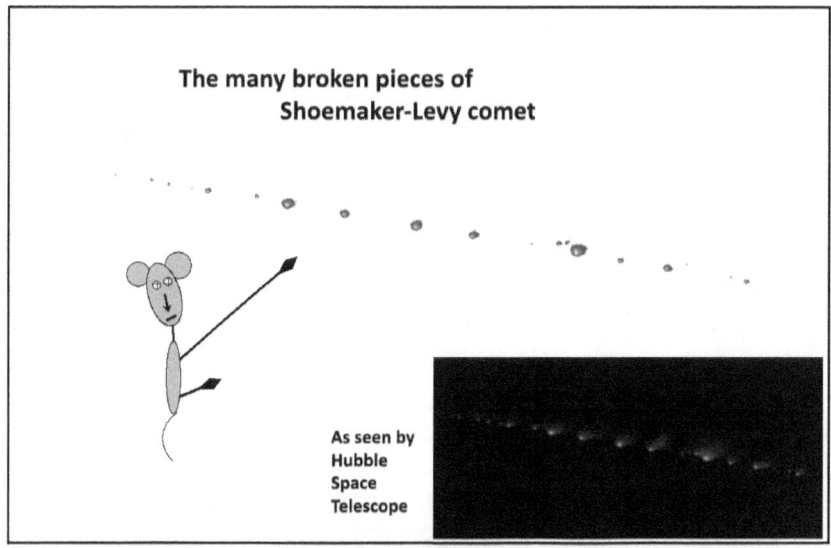

Some of the comets thrown earthward get captured in orbit around the sun and start to break apart into smaller fragments. We are familiar with this process, having seen and observed a number of such phenomena. The comet orbiting the sun breaks apart, first into a few pieces and then each piece breaks into more, until there are many pieces lined up in a row. That creates a structure in space resembling a celestial serpent's shape. The broken pieces of the Shoemaker-Levy comet are one such example as demonstrated by Mousy and Katzi in two different views.

The Shoemaker-Levy comet is about one mile in diameter and broke into twenty pieces. That is true for the typical comet, but there are other comet size possibilities in whatever the Oort Cloud or the Kuiper Belt sends earthward every 100,000 years. There could be more than one comet released, perhaps a group made of hundreds of comets like the Shoemaker-Levy comet coming earthward, getting captured around the sun and collectively breaking up into uncountable number of pieces. The canopy-building comet released earthward can likewise be a very large comet hundreds of miles in diameter. Such a large comet would then break into numerous pieces.

At this point let me stop and share an important point of view. What if I did not know about the Sermon on the Mount, had not received the divine whispers, and did not know about the knowledge of the canopied earth within the sacred texts and science records? Then, this whole talk of comets being released from the Oort Cloud or the Kuiper Belt, being captured by the sun, forming a cometary swarm of fragments through which the earth passes, and as a result builds a shell of cometary matter around the earth would be an interesting science fiction story, suitable for an episode in the Star Wars. Almost all of you reading my books fall into the category of skeptical disbelievers that would see the entertainment value in what I am saying about the canopied earth.

But what changes the situation and makes it an important piece of human reality is not that we have the Sermon on the Mount, or that the science community has gathered a huge database about remnants of the earth's experience of canopied earth, or that the sacred texts when read through the lens of the canopied earth become eyewitness accounts of the human experience encountering the cometary swarm, or least of all, my unprovable experience with divine whispers, but the aggregate of them all. When you put all the pieces together, the aggregate becomes undeniable evidence outlining a crucial aspect of human life.

With that, let me say goodbye to Mousy and Katzi and return them to their books. Let us continue the serious, though still brief account of the cometary swarm and the canopied earth. I start with the question: what are some exotic things that science knows about the canopied earth and you are hearing from me for the first time? Science has named one of its observations the Heinrich event. The signature of this event is layers of ice-rafted debris deposited in the North Atlantic Ocean's sediments. The deposits indicate massive discharges of iceberg armadas.[49,50] I repeat and I want you to imagine: huge armadas of icebergs. These are long trains of massive icebergs released at earth's North Pole and moving into the North Atlantic Ocean. How could that happen?

So long as we stay with the blue-skied version of the earth, there is no explanation for this phenomenon. Regardless of how hard science works, it cannot find the earthly factors that cause the iceberg armadas. Bring in the canopied earth, however, and it is quite easy to explain the phenomenon. You will read more about the iceberg armadas in my canopied earth books and I will not repeat that here. For now I want you to remain fascinated with the type of phenomena the humans will encounter in the canopied earth like the massive armadas of icebergs.

Testing what you know

I am a professor and love tests. So, at this point let me stop and test you. Here is the test. What is the scariest thing the human individual could possibly face? Is it the specter of blue-skied earth transitioning into canopied earth? Or something else? STOP and don't read anymore until you have your answer. If you said it is the canopied earth, you failed the test. The scariest thing to a human has always been "other humans," regardless of whether the earth remains blue-skied or canopied. This is the case even though it is a fact that the capabilities shared by others is the only way of sustaining the human individual's life.

So on one hand we need the societal sharing system where capabilities of others serve our daily needs and on the other hand, every one of us constantly seeks to protect oneself from other humans. If you disagree, have a closer look at the way we design our houses, our neighborhoods, our cities, and our nations, all intent on keeping us safe from "other humans." The events of the canopied earth can destroy the societal sharing system. Once the societal sharing system is gone, it is one human's brute force against the other humans. The brute force becomes the measure of obtaining what one needs for daily life. In such confrontation most will perish in the short run and all will be gone in the long run. It is the scary "other" that demands we do our best to maintain the societal sharing system under all circumstances, in all earth versions. We already have the divine suggestion that the best way of doing it is through adopting the Sermon on the Mount as the human way of life. It is a choice we have to think about most seriously.

Here is another test.

This time you are going to write a short essay about the two most important things that you need at eschaton. Remember, the eschaton is the transition from blue-skied to canopied earth. Those two most important things must be present at that moment. One is something that you must work hard to prepare and maintain.

The other, something for which you don't need to do anything. It is always present at the foundation of human life.

So don't read beyond this point if you are taking the test. However if you don't want to take the test and want to know the answer, then read on.

The first of the two most important things humans need when facing the eschaton is a "societal sharing system" based on the Sermon on the Mount. It is that certain way of capability sharing that will provide for everyone's needs regardless of the conditions they might face. Sharing of capabilities built on the Sermon on the Mount is the one that serves humans best in all times and conditions.

What is the second most important thing?

I am betting you missed this part of the test. I would be surprised if you did not. The second of the two most important things when facing the eschaton is "the divine." The divine being has been and will always be present in human life and will be most watchful of the human life in the eschaton condition. Here I have to add a word of warning as most of us do not see the divine as an aspect of the humankind and the universe but as an aspect of the religion business. If you think the divine will come to take care of those in the Catholic religion business, or those in the Protestant religion business, and would have no interest in other humans, you have no understanding of the Sermon on the Mount and the divine. You are too much of a customer in a religion business that has conditioned you to serve it.

The Sermon on the Mount is the clearest signal that the divine is for humankind, not for any select religion business. This view is contrary to the design and structure of every religion business. That is why for two thousand years the religion business has gone out of its way to dismiss and undermine the Sermon on the Mount as relevant to daily human life.

With that let me conclude the tests and go to the last chapter of this book.

XII

Elementary Observations

A friend regularly sends me valuable pieces of information. Here is one:

> When we think about God's plan for our lives, we often end up wondering about a different question entirely: What about our own plans for our lives? We fantasize about who we're supposed to marry, what job we're supposed to take, where we're supposed to live, or what other elements of life we should pursue for our happiness.[51]

This is a comparison of the power and wisdom of the divine and the human. One is tempted to consider the divine plan superior to any that humans put together on their own. To support that view often we search through the Bible to find verses that say we are born to serve God, therefore we must follow God's plan. Here is the problem. I am always intrigued that there is no such requirement in the Sermon on the Mount. We are not told that we are born to serve God. We are not told to make our plans subservient to those put forth by the divine. Instead, we are told we have a choice. We can build our life according to our own plan, or do so within the framework of God's plan in the beatitudes.

The divine position in the beatitudes is about the human that has been created as "choice maker." If the divine created the human as choice maker, by design, the divine would not tell the human what the human must do. The divine will only provide alternatives, like the way of life spelled out in the beatitudes. The human can choose to follow or not. Both ways are acceptable to the divine. Such is the way of the human created by the divine as "choice maker."

When I am complaining

I find it is easy to "complain." To complain requires minimal knowledge processing. It does little knowledge seeking and knowledge sharing. It uses the existing knowledge base and even that superficially and then lets loose with the complaint. Do you want to see me in the complaint mode? The following is one example where I caught myself complaining. It seems like I am saying a lot, but really saying little while playing with the popular suitcase words like government, market and competition.

Here we go. The complaint.

The Sermon on the Mount as life recipe cannot change the human as force applier and resource taker. Just as we are created as choice maker, we are created as force applier and resource taker. The human remains a resource taker whether or not following the Sermon on the Mount or any other life recipe. Given my current level of knowledge, I believe to succeed in aligning with the Sermon on the Mount, especially in initial stages, the society has to adopt small government and competitive markets. The small government minimizes the possibilities for application of brute force; the competitive markets push humans toward serving the needs of others for goods and services while taking minimum resources from them. Otherwise, the taking of resources and application of brute force will overtake and overwhelm the human behavior; no one's basic needs in daily life will be fully met and no one will pay attention to the beatitudes as way of life. Similarly, the noncompetitive market will take too much from the masses and not serve the masses, especially the excluded, as the focus of management will be on resource taking and applying concentrated force at first sign of a potential threat. The large government is always parasitic in structure and function and the prime tool of taking resources from the masses. The larger it gets, the more it deviates from serving the needs of the masses, especially in creating and maintaining a well-functioning force network. It should be obvious that the large government is always destructive with the out-of-proportion concentrated force it creates and uses.

End of the complaint.

How do the operational beatitudes, the first four steps, address the issues conveyed through my complaint? Is it in the first beatitude that we must address the knowledge-giving deficiencies that give rise to large government and non-competitive markets? Or should we see the large government and non-competitive markets as "mourning situations" to be brought up in the second beatitude? On the other hand, the large government and non-competitive markets are the best excuses for not paying attention to mourning situations. Everyone can hide behind the large government as solution provider or blame the dysfunctional market as creator and maintainer of mourning situations. By the time the society becomes dysfunctional in the first two beatitudes, the whole Sermon on the Mount would no longer matter. At that point, the third beatitude would be discarded as humans would not pay attention to alternatives as they constantly make the government larger in the hope that it will be a bigger solution provider. Also, the big government always acts as the killing machine that takes the resources of "outsider others," like other nations.

Finally, justice. It may come as a surprise, but the truth is that the large government and non-competitive market are "just" structures when viewed through the lens of the shared capabilities that maintain and sustain them. They are the best the society can put together and maintain with its knowledge base and capabilities. One may argue that such justice is deficient, that it fails to provide the goods and services for the daily needs of all, that it cannot stop destroying humans and their communities with application of intensely concentrated force or intense taking of resources, but that is how it is. Justice is an artifact defined by capabilities of those that make it. When not aligned with the beatitudes, humans can only address justice from a force-based point of view in which knowledge would only support and sustain the force-based system where the large government and non-competitive markets exist and operate.

I thought I had stopped complaining.

The challenge of many languages

In the process of understanding the divine knowledge, we often seem utterly ignorant of the fact that we are dealing with "translations." Translation always includes "interpretation." Interpretation always means the view of the translator entering the translation. Thus the purity of the original divine knowledge is always reduced through translation. Is this something bad? No. It is an inherent feature of understanding the divine knowledge. Humans speak many languages. The divine knowledge does not arrive in all languages. Many have to rely on translation in order to hear the divine words.

When dealing with translations, humans often engage in "moron behavior." The "moron behavior" is the behavior of those "not good in knowledge processing." It either rejects the divine knowledge because it has gone through multiple translations, or picks one specific translation and declares it to be exactly what the divine had said. Both, moronic behaviors. Both, behaviors of people bad in knowledge processing, people that lack the ability to understand how humans process, seek, and share knowledge. In the world of moronic behavior, some treat the divine as an ordinary human and wonder whether he spoke Aramaic, Greek, or both. Whether he actually sent his teachings to us in Greek or in Aramaic. Or, whether it was originally in Aramaic and St. Paul's religion business translated it into Greek because that was the main language of the market into which St. Paul wished to sell the products of his religion business. The moronic behavior often mixes the human and the divine.

The human, even though a knowledge processor, often forgets the basic human behavior in knowledge processing. If I am reading an article and come across a word I do not know, what do I do? I check the meaning of that word in a dictionary, then continue to read on. What happens if I am reading the Sermon on the Mount and come across a verse I do not understand? What should I do? There are multiple translations of the Sermon on the Mount. I can have look at different translations to see if by looking at multiple translations I develop a better understanding of what it says.

Assume I have looked at multiple translations and still the meaning is not clear. What do I do? There are detailed analyses of the Sermon on the Mount known as "commentaries." There are multiple commentaries on the Sermon on the Mount. I can read any or all of them in order to develop a better understanding. Assume I do that and access all shared knowledge of the society, and still find myself not understanding what the verse says? Now I am facing a "knowledge-giving deficiency" that has to be addressed through new knowledge seeking and knowledge sharing. In other words, I have reached a situation that requires I and others spend time and resources to seek new knowledge not currently available. Through knowledge seeking and sharing with others, sometime in the future, I will get to develop a better meaning for the verse that at present I do not fully understand. In short, looking back over decades and centuries many humans have done the hard work of translation. Many have done the hard work of developing commentaries. It is the individual human's task to make good use of the translations and commentaries in knowledge seeking and knowledge sharing when reaching for higher levels of understanding the divine knowledge.

It is important to note that not all translations and commentaries come with the same quality or attention to closeness of meaning to the original. Some translations and commentaries are quite intent at propagating the translator's or commentator's few-agree positions. All such differences are part of the challenges the human individual faces in knowledge processing. The Sermon on the Mount is not a freshly baked French baguette that we can place in our mouth and enjoy. It is something that we have to work hard to prepare before we can eat and enjoy it. The preparation comes through knowledge processing—the process of seeking and sharing knowledge. The prerequisite to understanding the Sermon on the Mount is to be good as knowledge processor. Should this come as a surprise or a burdensome requirement? No. We have faced the same situation in every course we have taken from kindergarten to college. In every course and in every subject the human cannot develop a good understanding if one is not a good knowledge processor—a good seeker and sharer of knowledge.

Foundation, not the same as structures that sit on top

It is important to note that the Sermon on the Mount is not a competitor to religious or political positions. It is not like asking those that really like Islam's religion business to switch to Buddhism, or Protestants to become Catholics. Every religion business is a human choice. The humans can choose to stay with what they like. This is no different than anyone can choose any car that one wants. The only suggestion is to engage in greater knowledge processing. Whether Catholic, Buddhist, Moslem, Protestant, or any other, the Sermon on the Mount is asking them all if they are aware of knowledge-giving deficiencies, and if aware, are they addressing them? Are they aware of the mourning situations and if so, are they addressing and removing them?

Note that even when we are aware that much of the sacred

texts are about the "canopied earth," still the human has the choice of seeing the canopied earth as the best manifestation of the divine and thus the best available model on how God becomes present in human life. I personally have no problem with such behavior. The human is the choice-maker, the knowledge processor, and the individual can engage in any choice making and knowledge processing so long as it does not result in application of brute force on others or adversely affect the flow of resources to others. In fact the purpose of the third and fourth beatitudes is just that—fair flow of resources and gentle application of force in the societal sharing system.

The same can be said about the political systems. Every society has its own choice of how it manages its politics, its way of concentrating brute force and extending it to create the laws; all a societal choice. One may declare the democratic design better; another may choose a monarchic design, and the other a dictatorial design. The Sermon on the Mount is neutral as to which design the society chooses. All the Sermon on the Mount highlights is the degree of dedication to having that system "be fair" and that fairness begins with identifying and addressing the knowledge-giving deficiencies and mourning situations and to patiently and gently considering the alternatives. The Sermon on the Mount is no threat to any religion business or government design, only a reminder of life fundamentals for humans as choice makers and knowledge processors. It tells everyone that they would be happier if they considered the Sermon on the Mount in their way of life, but it does not say one would not be happy using some other way of managing choice and knowledge, though it is implied that one would be happier with the Sermon on the Mount than without it.

Both governments and religion businesses come with a "bad" design on using brute force. Both are quite ready to apply brute force on others so they alone would survive, even if the survival means the utter destruction of many. This bad design will gradually fade away when using the Sermon on the Mount. Note that this bad design is not unique to the dictatorial government but includes all government designs be it democratic, socialist, or any other. They are all bad in reliance on brute force. The same is true of all religion businesses, whether Catholic, Protestant, or Islam. Throughout history they all come with an "apply brute force on others" label in all their products and services. Reliance on the Sermon on the Mount reduces the possibilities for the use of brute force and eventually, perhaps thousands of years from now, may even cause the religion businesses to abandon the brute force requirement like all other businesses that currently provide goods and services for daily human needs.

Searching for divine knowledge

It is valid to ask, how did I arrive at seeing the Sermon on the Mount as a foundational piece of knowledge? I think it started with a divine whisper but I am not sure. The divine whisper, so rare, so instantaneous and fleeting. The older I get the more I have trouble knowing when and how it happened. At times the most I remember is that it happened and in listening and responding to it I behaved in a different way.

As you read my books it should be obvious that I did not work on their material at the same time. I might work on the canopied earth for five years and then drop it and pay attention only to the force-based resource taking system. I recall the Sermon on the Mount had moved into the background and was not on my front burner when I met a woman with whom I had a conversation about the Bible and its foundational pieces. I recall she was adamant on paying attention to the Sermon on the Mount and so I did. I brought it back to the front. Now that I think about it, her behavior is what I would describe as a divine nudge. It was a short conversation, yet it brought back a different focus and priority to the Sermon on the Mount.

I have thought of and searched for other pieces of divine knowledge. I have considered the Sermon on the Plain and the Ten Commandments. I am writing books on both, but none has embedded itself in my mind as the Sermon on the Mount. Perhaps the Sermon on the Mount stands out among all pieces of divine knowledge because it integrates knowledge along all dimensions of human existence. It brings in the canopied earth, it brings in the force-based resource taking system, it brings in knowledge management, it tests the degree of learning this knowledge, and then makes us apply what we have learned to a variety of case studies to ensure that we've got it.

Some years ago, while thinking about the divine sources of knowledge I had made certain observations about the characteristics of the divine pieces of knowledge. I had thought about the ways that the human would get "divine knowledge" and saw three possibilities:

1. The human is actually in possession of a divine piece of knowledge applicable to every human, in every situation and for all times. (I see the Sermon on the Mount as one such divine knowledge.)

2. Since the divine knowledge has to flow through the social network that defines language and other patterns of human behavior, it would be affected by how it is seen and how it is deemed to be useful. In that case the divine knowledge gets modified to fit the perceived needs and circumstances of the moment and ceases to be a divine piece of knowledge. It now becomes a composite of divine and human knowledge and in the extreme turns into nothing but human-made knowledge. (I see most of the Gospels falling into this category of human-modified divine knowledge in order to make it fit the local time, circumstances and expectations.)

3. There is also the possibility that "human-made knowledge" gets declared as divine knowledge. This is the most treacherous form of knowledge as it conditions the human to see as divine knowledge something that definitely is not. It totally corrupts the social structure that sees such human knowledge as divine. (In this category the prime example is the letters of St. Paul, the executive letters that he wrote to

franchises in his business. For two thousand years, billions of humans have failed to see that these letters are human-made pieces of knowledge that have been declared by St. Paul's organization, namely the business we know today as Church, to be "divine knowledge." Those that fail to see "letters issued from corporate headquarters" and instead see the "word of God" face a serious problem in how they conduct their lives in interaction with others.)

This view will become more complex as we learn that the "divine knowledge," whether pure or mixed with human knowledge, comes in two versions: information about the human and human societies, and, information about the canopied earth. We would observe that humans have a strong tendency to present the canopy information as attributes of the divine being that delivers the divine knowledge. Thus in the sacred texts of today's societies, almost all divine attributes are canopy features assigned by humans who thought mixing the two would make the knowledge more relevant for their own time and circumstances. Only in rare occasions the sheer weight of the divine knowledge, as in the case of the Sermon on the Mount, would prevent the human from modifying it.

Revisiting to the opposition and the rejectionists

Reject and respect, but reject first. Does that work? At every act of judging the Sermon on the Mount it is first declared extraordinary, commanding respect, representing the truth of the divine message, but then rejected as the way of life, lowered to just moral and ethical talk before totally rejecting and setting it aside. Rejection is straightforward but why do we have to declare it extraordinary before rejecting? How do we know it is extraordinary? How do we know the words are the truth of the divine message for human life?

The perception of extraordinariness has led to an unending

stream of comments on the Sermon on the Mount. The comments come from all directions and styles but all end at the position that in the Sermon on the Mount the human deals with a piece of literature put together by the human. To be a bit nicer, give it some weight, they say it originated in Judaism. A group of people known as Jews brought it into existence to teach other humans about their select ways. Let us continue listening to this logic. Start with the Sermon on the Mount as a piece of literature and assume it is put together by a group of humans. More specifically, the Sermon on the Mount is a "collection of stuff" that forms a manual to teach the managers of an organization called the "Jesus movement." Instead of "manager," using the traditional terminology, we call these people "disciple." Instead of calling it a collection of stuff or manual we call it an *epitome*.[52] The dictionary tells us that epitome is a summary, abridgement, or abstract of a book, article or event.

Do you notice the subtlety of rejection? It is telling you that the Sermon on the Mount is not the direct words of the divine teaching but just an abridged and summarized version prepared as cheat sheets for managers of the Jesus movement to aid their memory of the divine teaching in whatever they do. In short, there is nothing divine about it. It may have originated at something that was divine knowledge but all we have is this abridged, summarized version prepared by humans for select use by other humans, those acting as organizational managers. Therefore, it is not the divine knowledge to be transmitted to the masses but pointers and hints at essential things to know and bear in mind by managers of the Jesus movement, the disciples.

I can only admire the subtlety of this type of rejection of the Sermon on the Mount. Even in rejection, the commentators cannot ignore the fact that the Sermon on the Mount does not seem to have been written for the select few but has a distinct universal character applicable to anyone. It has no requirements for being a Jew or Christian, or Buddhist or American before one can use the knowledge it gives to the human. Should that be surprising? Even though rejected or at best confined to the domain defined by the New Testament documents as the vehicle for preserving the

Sermon on the Mount, it remains a universal piece of knowledge addressed to humanity, far transcending the borderlines set by any religion or country. Perhaps this universal feature is the main underlying reason for its rejection. Every religion in the world is constructed as a "business" that wants to sell its brand of products to loyal customers. A universal piece of divine knowledge comes with the potential to destroy the religion business loyalty. The managers of every religion business would vehemently oppose such possibility as it would destroy their privileged managerial position. The Sermon on the Mount thus becomes alien to the way a religion business sets up and operates. Its divine origin is undermined and kept out of consideration. The religion business makes sure the Sermon on the Mount is rejected as anything valuable or having to do with the daily human life. The rejectionists recognize its extraordinariness when telling us that it originated at the divine teaching but destroy it by declaring that what has reached us is abridged and arranged in ways that has nothing to do with the divine or the masses of humans. To put a name behind this process, we are told that Matthew is the epitome's final author, who added his own ideas and views and edited the material as he saw fit for managers of Jesus movement.[53]

Here I face an immense dilemma. I am looking at two thousand years of history and tradition that tell me the Sermon on the Mount is an abridged manual of organizational instruction. Yet, instead of listening and obeying their pronouncement I continue to believe that the material in the Sermon on the Mount comes directly from the divine and is intended for every human on earth. The history and tradition clearly state that I am wrong, yet I stay with my own view even though at the end it might turn out to be only *my view*, everyone else continuing to reject the Sermon on the Mount and see it irrelevant for life, as done for thousands of years. I say the divine is speaking to the masses, the traditionalist says that, at best, it is speaking to the managers (disciples) who in turn might speak to others. The traditionalist would remind me that nowhere in the Sermon on the Mount says that it is the divine talking. All we are told is, "Here is what the divine said" and then are given the text of the Sermon on the Mount. While I see the reasoning behind the traditionalist view, I find it intriguing that Matthew never explicitly refers to the Sermon on the Mount in his gospel. It is as if he recognizes this is a "divine piece of knowledge" that must be delivered as is and it will speak on its own, on its own behalf, and there is no need to refer to it as no human reference can match what the divine is already delivering.

Is it possible that we have an intact piece of divine knowledge not altered and modified by humans to serve a specific religion business purpose? While I see Matthew transmitting the divine knowledge as the Sermon on the Mount, the tradition sees it as a text arranged, edited, and modified by Matthew from individual divine sayings on different occasions. We have already seen that humans, in their current level of knowledge, point at various coherency problems and defects in the Sermon on the Mount. Many of the purported incoherencies originate at the fact that the traditionalists cannot understand the multiple-choice tests in the Sermon on the Mount and cannot reconcile the choices in the test. All such perceived problems and inconsistencies are blamed on Matthew and in doing so the text gets further rejected as divine knowledge. It is declared just another piece of human knowledge even though in its beginning it might have touched upon a divine piece of knowledge. Such conclusions only point at human failure to recognize and manage the ignorance content inherent in whatever humans make and use.

Ignorance is a constant feature of human life. It manifests in a variety of ways. Often ignorance wears the mask of knowledge. For example, to mask the ignorance inherent in rejection of the Sermon on the Mount, the scholars have created an imaginary "Q-source" in which, supposedly, the real teachings of the divine resided. This is a nonexistent, unknown text that nonetheless is assumed to have existed and been the source from which someone like Matthew could put together the Sermon on the Mount. It is assumed that the Q-source could have existed in oral and written forms and maintained and transmitted by managers of the Jesus movement. So here, through the suitcase word "Q-source," we face another Sermon on the Mount rejection. Humans choose to create the imaginary, ignorance-riddled source for which we have no evidence of existence, then using this invisible construct they declare the Sermon on the Mount as writing done by Matthew using that imaginary source. Degrading and rejecting the Sermon on the Mount is the goal and is readily achieved through ignorance. All one needs is a single suitcase word like "Q-source" and the task is done. Now instead of learning from the Sermon on the Mount everyone would focus on methods of reconstructing an imaginary source like the Q-source.

A pessimistic view of capability

Humans have a strong tendency to forget that the government and societal sharing system are "artifacts" humans make and use. How humans make and use such artifacts depends completely on capabilities available and shared. The capabilities available, and the degree of capability sharing, vary noticeably from one society to the other and as such, there are distinct differences in governments and societal sharing systems formed. There is always the naïve assumption that a society can drop its government and societal sharing system and adopt another form of government and societal sharing system. Such assumption totally overlooks the role that the available and shared capabilities play in creation of the government and societal sharing system and the time and resources it takes to put together and operate a new form of government and societal sharing system. While humans regularly make this mistake with respect to the government and societal sharing system, they do not do so with any other artifact. For example, no one would entertain the notion of tearing down one's house assuming that another house can be built immediately in its place. No one assumes that throwing away one's wife and children will yield a better family the next day. We know whether it is a house, job, or family, it takes time and resources to bring it into existence, and replacing it with another not only might be beyond the capabilities one possesses but will take extra time and resources to accomplish, time and resources that if applied to the existing conditions could yield better results.

So what happens when a society decides to tear down its government and societal sharing system? We have learned that in human societies every government and societal sharing system begins at "brute force" as the foundation. The brute force is concentrated and extended to create the extended force network that sets the structure of rules and laws for human interactions, especially for capability sharing. If the extended force network is abandoned—thrown away—the society returns to the brute force domain and has to start with managing brute force first before it can extend it into new rules and laws to define the new modes of human interaction and capability sharing. There is no other alternative but brute force when the extended force network is torn apart and thrown away. As an example, listen to the following conversation and tell me what you see:[54]

> **Fareed**: For you Libya was in some ways heartbreaking to watch that country descend. Explain why.

> **Andrew**: I was in Libya in the late Gaddafi period and life under Gaddafi was worse than you can possibly imagine. It was a ridiculous place. It was unbelievably stressful. There was nothing to be said for the system that existed. But I made the mistake of thinking that if they got rid of the system which was so awful, that something better would have to rise in its place. And what happened instead was that it went into a state of complete chaos that even the patriotic Libyans I met when I was there had mostly tried to flee if they possibly can.

> Many people make the mistake of thinking that democracy and justice are the natural default state and if you remove all the impediments to these

qualities, that is what would rise up. And what I
learned as a personal lesson in dealing with Libya,
having argued that we should support the attacks
against Gaddafi, is that the normal state to which
people default is not democracy and is not order
but it is a terrifying, violent, brutal chaos.

What do you see? Two people, quite familiar with governments
and societal sharing systems, but having the lowest degree of
familiarity with "force management." They cannot see that any
society, whether Libya or the United States, if it abandons its
extended force network, it would end in the brute force domain.
Andrew who has experienced such transition, but lacks the
knowledge of force management, cannot say that after abandoning
its extended force network Libya "fell into the domain of brute
force." Instead, all he can say is how the domain of brute force
looked: terrifying, violent, brutal chaos.

More important in all this, we also fail to see that the Gaddafi
government was all that the people of Libya, with their capabilities
and with their ways of capability sharing, could put together.
They had no capability to put together a government in the style
of Britain, France, or the United States. In fact we don't have to
make such comparison at the level of government. We can say that
the people of Libya with their capabilities and with their ways of
capability sharing cannot put together automobile manufacturing
facilities as done in Britain, France, or the United States. They
cannot put together colleges and universities as done in Britain,
France, or the United States. In short, what any people can do
emerges from capabilities they have developed and the way they
share those capabilities. They can tear apart their existing factories
and in place of destroyed factories they can never create automobile
manufacturing facilities in the manner of Britain, France, or the
United States. They can tear apart and destroy their educational
institutions and in their place they can never create colleges and
universities in the manner of Britain, France, or the United States.
All they would get from destruction of their existing artifacts is

life in the brute force domain. The humankind is yet to learn this simple force management fact of life. We keep destroying in the hope of finding something better when the path should be that of focusing on knowledge seeking and knowledge sharing to develop capabilities and how they are shared.

A serious problem

At this moment in time, I often consider myself the human most familiar with the knowledge-based message of the Sermon on the Mount, yet often I find myself acting in ways not aligned with the Sermon on the Mount. For example, the Sermon on the Mount is about knowledge-based life—life of addressing knowledge-giving deficiencies, life of identifying potential and existing mourning situations and addressing them. It is a life of searching among patient and gentle alternatives and being totally dedicated to pursuit of fairness in human interactions. Yet at watching something as simple as a game I fail to do so. I take sides for no reason. I cheer my side winning and moan in pain when it is losing. Why do I choose the alternative of behaving in a way that not only comes with the possibility of pain for me but guarantees my joy will be at the expense of someone else's pain? It is not that there is no other way of generating joy from watching a game. I can definitely enjoy the actions and skills of players on both sides. I can moan and groan at lost opportunities and bad plays of all players. But I don't do that. Is it because "choosing sides" is a simple way of creating possibilities for pain and suffering? Does that mean we humans like and enjoy pain and suffering, especially when inflicted on others? Is this a result of how humans manage their few-agree and many-agree positions? Is this a sign of humans trapped in a force-based system that always demands opposition that inevitably produces pain and suffering? Even in situations where one cannot choose sides between two competing teams, like ballet, still the storyline declares one dancer as the good guy and the other as the bad guy and we tend to take the side of the one that has been declared good rather than focus on knowledge-giving deficiencies or ways of artifact making that create both sides in life.

Why am I highlighting this? Perhaps the millennia-old rejection of the Sermon on the Mount is not just an accident of not understanding what it says. Perhaps there is something in human behavior and design that makes us become "side takers" first before we act as "knowledge processors." This can be no different than humans acting as force appliers and resource takers. Both the force applier and resource taker are a constant challenge to the knowledge-based way of the Sermon on the Mount. The "side taking" could be an even bigger challenge. Perhaps we need to start with the human as side taker, resource taker, and force applier. Perhaps side taking is an inherent feature of applying force and taking resources.

When applying brute force on others, the first thing we do is to take sides. When we take resources, the first thing we do is to take sides. Thus managing "side taking" is as significant as managing the force application and taking of resources. In fact the most apparent place for side taking is in the second beatitude when we are asked, "can you mourn?" In effect, we are asked, "can you not take sides?" We often do not mourn—cannot recognize pain and suffering of others simply because they are not on "our side." When the bombs are dropping on a city full of humans, we show no interest in understanding their mourning situation because we have already declared that they are on the "enemy side" and they deserve all the mourning situations they can get. So behaving in the knowledge-based way of the Sermon on the Mount requires managing our "side taking" tendencies. From observing my own behavior I can tell you, that is not an easy thing to do.

The side-taking can also be an outcome of the "loss management" way of life adopted today by all societies. No human likes "loss," whether it is personal like losing a loved one or resource-based like losing wealth. The same pattern exists at the societal level. Assume we do not identify and address the individual and societal losses through identifying and addressing knowledge-giving deficiencies. If all we do is face the continual parade of losses, then the human as choice maker would emphasize side-taking in order to see and experience only part and not all of the losses. Whether in family, workplace, community or society, the human individual would choose the side that in one's opinion would minimize the potential losses. Thus even in the simplest human encounters, namely a game, instead of observing and enjoying the skills exhibited by both sides, we take one side that would most likely be the winner and desire that it become loss-less while those taking the other side would mourn the pain and suffering of the losses. So long as we are in the loss management way of life we have to choose the side that avoids loss. In the loss management way of life the side-taking is the only way of improving one's position, even though at the final count the society built on loss management will lose as eventually the brute force of oppositional side-taking will destroy the whole society. As choice makers we are stuck with taking sides so long as the society is structured on the basis of loss management and not on identifying and addressing the knowledge-giving deficiencies.

Let me take a step back and have another look at side taking from a different angle. The human is "good-not good decision maker" which makes him or her a choice maker. The bad part of being a choice maker is that the human also becomes a "side taker" and side taking almost always carries with it the potential for confrontation and eventually the possibility for application of brute force by one side on the other. Sadly this makes choosing or rejecting the Sermon on the Mount an act of "side taking." Those that choose it as way of life have to be ready to face the opposition and persecution by those who have chosen another way and not the way of the Sermon on the Mount. That is the sad conclusion of side taking.

The side taking is the same as "boundary drawing." Humans are "boundary drawers." They especially draw the boundaries that define "life." Within the chosen boundary they allow life; outside it, they destroy life. Such arrangement is applied to all life forms, including the human life. Whether the boundary is drawn at home or at nation as to which life forms (human or bug) are allowed into the house or nation and which ones will be destroyed if entering the house or nation, it is the boundary that both defines and destroys life. Boundary-drawing, as an outcome of managing force and resources, remains a serious aspect of human life. If humans constantly set oppositions bent on destruction of life we can rightly conclude that humans, in addition to being "force applier" and "resource taker," are also "self-destroyer." Remembering the "water bottle example" as to how human lives are interlinked through shared capabilities, the more "opposition" one creates, the more one engages in acts of self-destruction. In terms of societally shared capabilities, the purpose of every opposition is to destroy self. The self and opposition are destructively linked. If humans are self-destroyers and otherwise cannot manage life, we are left with the inevitable conclusion that no divine recipe, like the Sermon on the Mount, will make any difference in how humans conduct life. They will destroy themselves whether or not they are aligned with the divine knowledge.

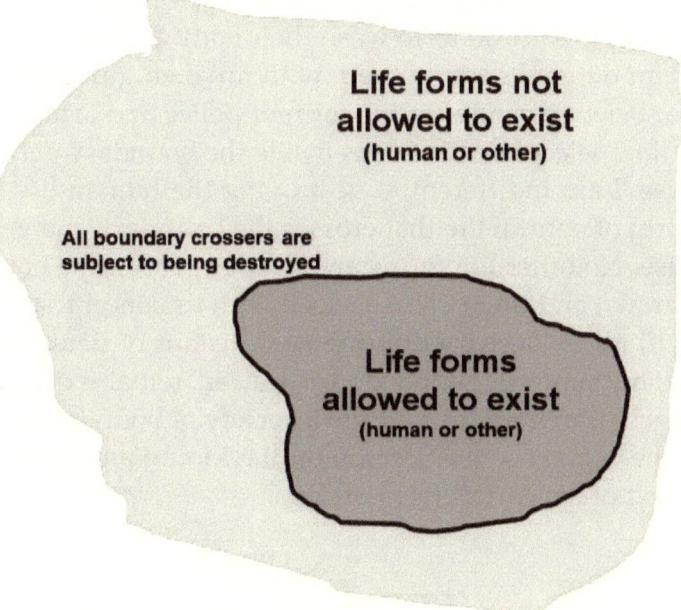

There is no doubt that humans are "boundary drawers," but does this originate in managing the human as force applier and resource taker? Does it originate in how humans manage the few-agree and many-agree positions in life? Does being a force applier require drawing boundaries outside of which brute force will be applied on others? Does being a resource taker require drawing a boundary beyond which resources of others will be taken regardless of what the others think of such resource taking? Regardless of how we understand the human as "boundary drawer," the biggest adverse impact of boundaries is on "life" itself. We often draw boundaries where natural life can or cannot exist. The bug can exist outside the home, but will certainly be destroyed if it crosses from the outside into the home and gets detected. Such behavior is not limited to life forms like bugs. We certainly draw boundaries where human life will not be allowed to exist. My house is one such boundary inside which I exclude almost all of humanity. I will not allow any of billions of humans to come and use one of my extra bedrooms to sleep and rest, or use the food in the refrigerator to relieve their hunger, or use one of my multiple bathrooms to wash their body and clean up. I will keep them out and destroy them with my own gun or the guns that the society provides in the form of police and armed forces. I only allow select few life forms inside the boundary defined by my house. I am indifferent to destroying the human life or any other form of natural life that crosses the boundary and gets into my house. No other life forms are allowed within the boundary I have drawn and the society backs it with its concentrated force. They will all be destroyed at the first instant of detection. The reality of my existence as "boundary drawer" remains distinct and unchanged. Can humans manage a society of boundary-drawers within the context of the Sermon on the Mount and then within the context of the earth's two versions?

Surviving while everyone else is losing

Here I want to introduce to you a very specific and somewhat odd group of boundary drawers. They are humans that see the whole societal sharing system made of losers and want to remain among the few winners outside it. These humans see everyone getting vaporized in the shower of nuclear weapons and only they, hiding someplace underground, survive to become the humanity again. They are the "hole-dwellers." They see hole-dwelling as the winning strategy in a life of boundary-drawers.

The "society of hole-dwellers" are people that assume they can gather and stockpile some goods produced by the society's capability sharing system, then dig a hole in the ground and go and hide in it. To them such life strategy is better than continuing to work to maintain the balance in the force-based resource taking system to prevent brute force confrontations. They have lost any interest in maintaining the capability sharing system so that everyone receives the goods and services they need in life. For them the capability sharing system is a goner.

Consider a thought experiment in today's societal sharing system. Assume everyone stops working, no one sharing capabilities with others to produce goods and services for all. What does that do? It turns a society of capability sharers into a society of hole-dwellers. We all have to find and gather things as soon as we can and then go and hide somewhere, hoping that we will survive the absence of the societal sharing system. Our houses turn into "holes" in which we hide and there we protect what we have gathered with brute force against intruders that have run out of things and want to get what we have. Inevitably a society of hole-dwellers is a society of force appliers. Everyone, sooner or later, runs out of things in the hole and in order to get whatever one needs, one has to confront others with brute force. This makes the society of hole-dwellers a society of harm-throwers.

The end point of the society of harm-throwers is always the destruction of all. The society of capability sharers is the only way of avoiding the destruction of all, yet no society has learned this lesson well. Every society seeks to become the best force-applier ever, the best harm-thrower ever. Every human always thinks in terms of surviving in the destruction-dedicated society of force appliers by becoming a hole-dweller that kills all others in order to stay alive. The movies regularly portray such humans as the *hero* of the human societies.

The humans, the choice makers, would they choose to be the capability sharers to serve the needs of all? Or, pick a small piece of the societal sharing system and crawl into a hole? It is a sad story to see the capability-sharers become the hole-dwellers, but even the divine would see it a choice. At the final count it is the choice maker that defines the human way of life.

Endnotes

1   W. D. Davies and Dale C. Allison, Jr., <u>The Gospel According to Saint Matthew</u>, Vol. 1 (T. T. Clark, 1988), pp. 429-430.

2   In this book all verses of the Sermon on the Mount come from the King James Version of the Bible.

3   Hans Dieter Betz, <u>The Sermon on the Mount</u> (Fortress Press, 1995), p. 111.

4   Liviu Barbu, "The 'poor in spirit' and our life in Christ: an Eastern Orthodox perspective on Christian discipleship," <u>Studies in Christian Ethics</u> 22(3) 261–274 (2009).

5   Ulrich Luz, <u>Matthew 1-7: A Continental Commentary</u>, trans. W. C. Linss, (Fortress Press, 1989), p. 232.

6   Erickson, Millard J, <u>Introducing Christian doctrine</u>, 2nd ed., Arnold Hustad, ed. (Baker Book House, 1992), pp. 262, 266, 270.

7   John R. W. Stott, <u>The message of the Sermon on the Mount</u> (Inter-Varsity Press, 1978), p. 33.

8   I am assuming you have read my other books and are familiar with the earth's two versions. If not, one version is blue-skied like today's earth, the other version has a shell of cometary matter around it and is called the canopied earth. Science knows the two versions as interglacial and glacial. The interglacial lasts around 15,000 years, the glacial 85,000 years and the two together set a 100,000-year cycle that repeats.

9   John R. W. Stott, <u>The message of the Sermon on the Mount</u> (Inter-Varsity Press, 1978), p. 33.

10 Adam Smith, <u>Lectures on Jurisprudence</u> (Liberty Classics, 1982), p. 340.

11 <u>Luther's Works: The Sermon on the Mount and the Magnificat</u>, Vol. 21, ed. Jaroslav Pelikan (Concordia Publishing House, 1956), p. 285.

12 Ibid, p. 3.

13 Hans Dieter Betz, <u>The Sermon on the Mount</u> (Fortress Press, 1995), pp. 94-95.

14 Ibid, p. 105.

15 Joseph Ratzinger, Pope Benedict XVI, <u>The divine of Nazareth</u> (Doubleday, 2007), p. 80.

16 Ibid, p. 86

17 Ibid, p. 87.

18 Ibid, P. 93

19 Ibid, p. 80.

20 Ibid, p. 82.

21 Ibid, p. 103.

22 Ibid, p. 97

23 Hans Dieter Betz, <u>The Sermon on the Mount</u>, A. Y. Collins, ed. (Fortress Press, 1995), p. 111.

24 All bible verses in this book come from the King James Version.

25 Hans Dieter Betz, <u>The Sermon on the Mount</u>, A. Y. Collins, ed. (Fortress Press, 1995), p. 111.

26 Ibid., pp. 113-116.

27 Ibid., p. 117.

28 Ibid., p. 123.

29 Ibid.

30 Ibid.

31 Harvey K. McArthur, <u>Understanding the Sermon on the Mount</u> (Greenwood Press, 1960), chapter 4.

32 "Unpacking Suitcase Words," http://alexvermeer.com/unpacking-suitcase-words/.

33 Mario Pei, <u>Weasel Words: The Art of Saying What You Don't Mean</u> (Harper and Row, New York, 1978).

34 Philip Meyer, "Trailing a weasel word," <u>Columbia Journalism Review</u> <u>28</u> (5), 10-11 (Jan./Feb. 1990).

35 "Weasel word," http://en.wikipedia.org/wiki/Weasel_word.

36 Adam Smith, <u>The Wealth of Nations</u> (Bantam, 2003), pp. 338-339.

37 The question concerns the application of human wisdom to divine wisdom to determine the correctness of the order of the second and third beatitudes. See Hans Dieter Betz, <u>The Sermon on the Mount</u>, A. Y. Collins, ed. (Fortress Press, 1995), pp. 124-125.

38 The gospels that contain the beatitudes have reached us in different versions. In most versions the sequence of the first four beatitudes is the same as what the gospels show today. But there are some manuscripts in which the positions of the second and thirds beatitudes are switched. Those that were copying and producing the manuscripts must have felt the proper order should be the meek first and then the mourning. This logic basically says: look at alternatives to deficiencies in knowledge giving and do so gently without application of force. After you become good at gentle assessment of deficiencies in knowledge giving in all ordinary levels, then consider the mourning situations in which reside the extreme knowledge-giving deficiencies. This logic lacks the urgency of addressing the mourning situations. It would direct "patience," meaning lots of time, at situations where humans face very bad cases of pain and suffering, the extremes of knowledge-giving deficiencies. The "can you mourn?" emphasizes the fact that as soon as we are "aware" of deficiencies in knowledge giving, our focus should be directed at addressing and removing extremes of knowledge-giving deficiencies as no one can be left in extreme pain and suffering for long. Only then, after having taken care of the mourning situation, does one return to gentle assessment of alternatives in human life. To me, not only does this makes human sense, in all the divine whispers and nudges I have experienced I never felt anything that pointed at the beatitudes having a different order.

39 Karen Lebacqz, <u>Six theories of justice</u> (Augsburg, 1986).

40 Hans Dieter Betz, <u>The Sermon on the Mount</u>, A. Y. Collins, ed. (Fortress Press, 1995), pp. 200-201.

41 Ibid., p. 215.

42 Ibid., p. 217.

43 Ibid., p. 219.

44 Ibid., p. 215.

45 Ibid., p. 330.

46 Ibid., p. 423.

47 Ibid., p. 520.

48 Ibid., p. 360.

49 Heinrich, H., "Origin and consequences of cyclic ice rafting in the northeast Atlantic Ocean during the past 130,000 years," <u>Quaternary Research</u> <u>29</u>, 142-152 (1988).

50 Bond, G., Heinrich, H., Broecker, W., Labeyrie, L., McManus, J., Andrews, J., Huon, S., Jantschik, R., Clasen, S., Simet, C., Tedesco, K., Klas, M., Bonani, G., Ivy, S., "Evidence for massive discharges of icebergs into the North-Atlantic ocean during the last glacial period," <u>Nature</u> <u>360</u>, 245-249 (1992).

51 David Loewer, private communication, April 19, 2017.

52 Hans Dieter Betz, <u>The Sermon on the Mount</u>, A. Y. Collins, ed. (Fortress Press, 1995), pp. 76-77.

53 Ibid., pp. 23, 81.

54 The conversation is between Fareed Zakaria of *Fareed Zakaria: GPS* and Andrew Solomon, author and foreign correspondent. CNN, June 26, 2016.

www.ingramcontent.com/pod-product-compliance
Lightning Source LLC
Chambersburg PA
CBHW030440290526
45786CB00001B/368